SIMPLE DISHES THAT LOOK AFTER THEMSELVES

FROM THE OVEN TO THE TABLE

DIANA HENRY

MITCHELL BEAZLEY

CONTENTS

INTRODUCTION

Closing the oven door and swinging a tea towel over my shoulder is one of the most satisfying movements I make in the kitchen. I love the alchemy that takes place behind that door. It's astonishing how heat, on its own—without you directing it or supervising it very much—can turn simple ingredients into a meal.

Because I love cooking, I'm happy to make complicated food; I know that some dishes can only be achieved by browning the constituent elements and slowly building layers of flavor. There will never come a time when I don't want to cook and eat *boeuf bourgignon*, a dish that needs this kind of attention. But I can't cook food like this from Monday to Thursday, I just don't have the time. If you're a throw-it-in-the-oven kind of cook, whether by necessity or desire, then this book is for you.

The dish that introduced me to this laid-back oven-loving approach was an Antonio Carluccio recipe for chicken thighs cooked with little potatoes, red onion wedges, garlic, rosemary, and olive oil. When I discovered it—it's in his book *An Invitation to Italian Cooking* —I silently mouthed the word "genius" and knew that I had stumbled across something life-changing. For that dish, you don't brown anything, you just put the ingredients in a roasting pan, season them, put them in the oven, and wait for 45 minutes. Then you eat. It's still the meal I have cooked more than any other over the last 20 years.

In that time, I've built up a repertoire of dishes on this theme, some with a layer of stock poured underneath the meat; as the dish cooks the top becomes golden and a sauce develops below. I worked out how to apply this approach to rice instead of potatoes, the stock reducing and being absorbed as the grains cook to tenderness. I roast foods that are more usually done in a pan on the stovetop—sausage, broccoli, and salmon fillets—just because I think it's easier. It is literally "hands off" cooking.

Why is it important, when I know that cooking does take effort, to offer you dishes that, while requiring attention, are relatively easy to achieve? Because I believe that the table is important. I wouldn't have managed to feed my children well and share food with friends (on a Wednesday as well as on a Saturday night) without finding simple ways to do things. The dishes that follow—from cozy sausages baked with tomatoes, potatoes, and pecorino cheese, to a celebratory dish of sea bass with a Middle Eastern stuffing—have helped.

Because I roast and bake so much, I've amassed loads of roasting pans, baking sheets, gratin dishes, and two broad shallow casseroles (though, truthfully, you only need one).

I'm not the only person who likes this kind of cooking. There are scores of American books devoted to "sheet pan cooking." We're not so familiar with sheet pans in the UK, but they're a great invention: heavy-gauge baking sheets with a lip around them. If you have sheet pans, you can use them instead of roasting pans for many of the dishes in this book.

You don't need lots of new pans to cook the food that follows, but it's a good idea to read the section on equipment.

In the UK, people have started to call these dishes—cooked in roasting pans or sheet pans—"tray bakes," a term I just can't use, because, when I was growing up, tray bakes were exclusively sweet. Brownies, blondies, lemon bars… these were "tray bakes," so you won't find the term used here.

Many of the recipes that follow are for one-pot meals, but not all of them. When I have been able to incorporate a starch, I have. With some, I just wanted to give you a basic roast. With others, I felt that an accompanying grain, bread, or salad was what you needed. There are no pasta dishes baked from raw in a roasting pan, as I hate the texture that produces. Pasta—like bulgur wheat—is actually easier to make on the stovetop, anyway.

So that you don't have to consult other books when cooking out of this one, I've included a page on how to cook various grains, and two pages on how to cook potatoes and sweet potatoes in the oven in lots of different ways alongside whatever else you are roasting.

Where the dishes are one-pot, they vary in terms of effort. The most basic really do just require you to chuck ingredients in a pan, season them, and roast them. At the other end of the scale—as in a smoked fish, tomato, and potato gratin, for example—you have to slice potatoes thinly and heat cream and milk before pouring it into the gratin dish. Some recipes are for fairly plain roasts that are made more special by a relish or a salsa on the side. You can choose whether to make the relish or not (I have suggested simpler accompaniments that you can buy), and there are also two pages of relish recipes that only require you to mix or chop, so you can change things up.

To cook this way—using very simple methods—you do need a well-stocked pantry. You're not doing much to the food you're cooking, so you need big flavors. There are ingredients—pomegranate molasses, miso, preserved lemons—that you need to get. A lot of unusual foods that weren't available even five years ago are now sold in supermarkets, but if you don't have a good one near you, everything can be ordered online. I grew up in a small town where many things were impossible to buy. I wish we'd had the access to ingredients we do now. Delivery costs are an issue, but put together a list of things you need and then order them together, so you only have one delivery fee.

You don't just roast in the oven, of course, you also pot-roast, bake, and do what some cookbooks refer to as "wet roast." I've written more about these later in the book. (There's not much science, just enough to help.) I do love what the application of dry heat—proper roasting—does to food, though, the way it caramelizes the surface of meat and the edges of vegetables. This heat can even help a batch of under-ripe and cottony apricots: roasted with a light dusting of sugar, the heat intensifies everything that is hidden when they're raw. It finds their sweetness, chars spots on their flesh, makes them tender and mouth-puckeringly tart.

Ovens used to have more of a physical presence in the home. Roasting and baking was done on an open hearth, not in a closed box with a glass front. Snowed in one year in Friuli in Northern Italy, I discovered the *fogolar*, a raised cooking area in the middle of the kitchen or living room with a chimney above it. Everyone gathered round this to get warm while the snow kept us prisoner, but it also provided many of our meals. It's convenient to have the oven against the wall in modern kitchens, tucked away, closed off, slick with dials. But it doesn't give it the status it deserves. In my mind, and in my cooking, the oven is central.

COOKING EQUIPMENT

Do you need any fancy pieces of equipment to cook from this book? Nope. But a few roasting pans are, obviously, a must-have (that way you can roast more than one dish in the oven at the same time). Some of mine have been on the go for thirty years, and the more bashed and worn they become, the more I love them. You need a heavier-gauge pan that you can use on the stovetop as well as in the oven (essential for reducing cooking juices), and a few lighter ones. Lighter-weight pans are often not suitable for using over direct heat, though, as they buckle, so choose the roasting pan according to what you're going to do with it. A mixture of sizes is important. You'll notice that I often suggest the components of a dish "lie snugly" together. That's because if there's a lot of room around food that's roasting, the juices will evaporate and can, if they're in the oven long enough, burn. In lots of the recipes, the ingredients have to lie in a single layer (because if they lie on top of each other they sweat or steam rather than browning), so you need a very large roasting pan—or two medium-sized pans—that will hold everything. Roasting and baking are simple, but you have to follow the instructions.

I hate being didactic—many recipes are just blueprints on which you can put your own stamp—but the food won't turn out well if you don't pay attention to the size of the dish, if one is specified. This is especially the case if the recipe contains stock or cream; it has been tested so that a specific quantity of liquid will reduce to the right amount in the time and at the temperature given. The size of the cooking vessel will affect this.

I also have a few sheet pans. These have lips around them of varying depths, but always shallower than the sides of roasting pans. They're really useful and usually lighter than roasting pans.

The other essential is a shallow casserole or braiser. Many of the recipes in the book have been tested and cooked in the dishes I use most often, a couple of 12in shallow casseroles. I have one that is made of carbon steel and is 2in deep. The other is cast iron, made by Chasseur, and is 2½in deep. You can serve out of them as well as cook in them (though I don't object to serving out of a roasting pan; there's one on my table right now). Staub and Le Creuset also make enameled cast iron versions in the correct size, but they're expensive (Le Creuset is now pretty much unaffordable). There are cheaper options, though. Lodge makes a cast-iron skillet that is the right size and depth for forty dollars, though you will need to season it before using. Paella pans—make sure to get one that, again, is 12in across—can be bought for twenty dollars or less, though of course you have to be sure that the quality is good. Make sure, too, that the pan doesn't have plastic-covered handles, as they can't go in the oven. A ceramic dish with a capacity of two quarts is useful for the baked desserts that are in the "Something Sweet" chapter.

Some gratin dishes—the ones used in the book are made of enamel or cast iron and have capacities of one and two quarts—are important too, as well as a frying pan that can be used on the stovetop and in the oven (so it shouldn't have a plastic or a wooden handle, or a non-stick coating).

I'm not keen on gadgets, but I do have good knives, a zester, a citrus juicer, a mandolin for slicing potatoes thinly (you need this for only one dish in this book, though a good sharp knife will also do the job, albeit more slowly), and a mortar and pestle. A mortar and pestle, though old-fashioned, is sometimes better than a food processor, especially for bashing toasted spices and for making chunky relishes.

A CUPBOARD TO LOVE

Gone are the days when a home had a larder or pantry, a huge storage space packed with myriad possibilities to help you make dinner: cans and jars of preserved goods, spices, all manner of grains and legumes. Now we mostly have built-in cupboards, often so deep that you give up trying to find the ingredient you know is in there.

Because I grew up in a small town where it was impossible to find unusual ingredients, one of my greatest pleasures is stocking up with interesting bits and pieces, and I love cooking with them. Bags and jars of foods used in Japan or Korea or Sicily bring new experiences as well as dinner.

When you cook using simple methods—such as roasting—the interest often comes from the ingredients you add to a pan of chicken thighs or salmon fillets. Here, then, are the things it would be useful to have on hand when you're cooking from this book. You don't need to have them all at the same time, but if you're putting a selection together—or want to make an online order—bear these in mind. (And, for suppliers, *see* page 234.)

OILS AND VINEGARS Extra virgin olive oil, peanut oil, toasted sesame oil, cider vinegar, white balsamic vinegar, sherry vinegar, unseasoned rice vinegar

CANS AND JARS Anchovies, unsweetened coconut milk and coconut cream, canned tomatoes, black and green olives, preserved lemons, pickled chilies, capers, pickles, crystallized ginger

CONDIMENTS, PASTES, AND SAUCES White and red miso paste, harissa, pomegranate molasses, light and dark soy sauces, chili sauce (such as sriracha), Thai fish sauce, tahini, Dijon mustard, chipotle paste, tamarind paste, *gochujang* hot pepper paste, mayonnaise, tomato paste, *kecap manis* (Indonesian soy sauce)

SPICES Cumin and coriander (both ground and seeds), chili flakes or crushed red pepper, Hungarian sweet, Hungarian sharp and Spanish smoked paprika, saffron, cardamom, turmeric, fennel seeds, cinnamon (ground and sticks), bay leaves, cayenne pepper, black peppercorns, caraway, ginger, nutmeg, sea salt flakes

GRAINS AND LEGUMES Basmati rice, Spanish paella rice, short-grain rice, Puy lentils, freekeh, couscous, bulgur wheat, barley, cans of white beans (cannellini and haricot) and black beans, dried haricot and cannellini beans, canned chickpeas, pouches of pre-cooked lentils and grains (such as freekeh, barley, and mixed grains)

NUTS, SEEDS, AND DRIED FRUITS I tend to buy nuts as I need them because some—walnuts, for instance—turn rancid quite quickly, but these are what I always have in my kitchen: flaked almonds, blanched almonds, ground almonds, blanched hazelnuts, shelled unsalted pistachios, roasted unsalted peanuts, vacuum-packed cooked chestnuts, white sesame seeds, raisins, dried sour cherries, prunes, dried cranberries

SWEET THINGS Honey, maple syrup, dark and light brown sugars, palm sugar, superfine and granulated sugar

ALCOHOLS Amaretto, Marsala, amontillado sherry, dark rum, dry white vermouth, crème de cassis

BAKING Rose and orange flower waters, all-purpose flour, instant polenta, confectioners' sugar, good-quality marzipan, dark chocolate (70% cocoa solids), cocoa powder, vanilla beans or vanilla extract, baking powder, baking soda

SIMPLE SUPPERS

SAUSAGES, CHOPS,
FISH FILLETS & THE LIKE

BAKED SAUSAGES, APPLES & BLACKBERRIES WITH MUSTARD & MAPLE SYRUP

I know it's in the "Simple Suppers" chapter, but this—glossy with blackberry juice and maple syrup—is special enough to serve to friends on weekends. I roast sausages all the time. Sometimes I brown them a little in a pan before transferring them to the oven; sometimes I just put them in the oven raw, moistened with a little oil, and turn them halfway through cooking. Either way is infinitely less hassle than standing turning them over in a pan on the stovetop.

Preheat the oven to 400°F.

Tumble the sausages, apples, onions, and rosemary into a heavy flameproof roasting pan, shallow casserole, or ovenproof frying pan about 12in across, in which the ingredients can lie snugly in a single layer. There shouldn't be a lot of room around the ingredients or the juices will reduce and burn.

In a small bowl, stir together the maple syrup, mustard, olive oil, and garlic, then pour this mixture into the pan. Season and turn the ingredients to coat them. Bake for 40–50 minutes, turning over the sausages once. They should be dark and glossy, with the apples completely soft.

Remove the dish or pan from the oven and place over medium-high heat, pouring in the stock. Bring almost to a boil, stirring to help the maple syrup and mustard mixture melt into the stock. Add the blackberries to heat through (don't stir from now on, or they will break up) and serve with mashed or baked potatoes.

SERVES 4

8 good-quality chunky pork sausages

2 tart apples, halved (no need to peel or core)

2 medium onions, each cut into 6–8 wedges

2 rosemary sprigs

3½ tablespoons maple syrup

1½ tablespoons Dijon mustard

1 tablespoon extra virgin olive oil

2 garlic cloves, crushed

sea salt flakes and freshly ground black pepper

⅔ cup chicken stock

6oz blackberries

mashed or baked potatoes, to serve

ROAST SALMON & STRING BEANS WITH CORNICHONS & MUSTARD CRUMBS

They're not cheap, but salmon fillets do mean an easy supper, as they cook so quickly. Roast string beans were a revelation to me the first time I tried them (American chef and lover of vegetables Joshua McFadden, got me into them). If you want to serve these beans as a side dish, roast them as directed here, scattering the flavored crumbs over them at the end (and for more roast string beans, see pages 64 and 88).

see pages 64 and 88

Preheat the oven to 400°F.

Put the string beans into a roasting pan or—even better—a shallow ovenproof dish that you would want to serve from, too. Toss them with a little of the oil and some seasoning.

Brush the salmon fillets with oil as well, season, then set them on top of the beans. Roast for 12 minutes.

Heat the remaining oil in a frying pan on the stovetop. When it's hot, add the breadcrumbs and fry briskly until golden, then add the garlic and cornichons and cook for another minute. Take the pan off the heat and stir in the mustard, parsley, and lemon zest, mixing together well.

When 2 minutes of cooking time remain, spoon the breadcrumb mixture on top of the salmon and return it to the oven.

Squeeze the lemon juice over the top of the fish and serve.

SERVES 4

1lb 2oz string beans, stem end removed

4 tablespoons extra virgin olive oil

sea salt flakes and freshly ground black pepper

4 salmon fillets, 6–7oz each

¾ cup breadcrumbs from coarse white bread (such as ciabatta or sourdough)

1 garlic clove, finely grated

3 tablespoons drained and chopped cornichons

2 teaspoons Dijon mustard

2 tablespoons finely chopped flat-leaf parsley leaves

finely grated zest and juice of ½ unwaxed lemon

TOAD IN THE HOLE WITH SCALLIONS & CHEDDAR CHEESE

SERVES 4

3 extra-large eggs

generous 1 cup all-purpose flour, sifted

½ cup whole milk

½ cup beer

1 tablespoon English mustard

sea salt flakes and freshly ground black pepper

3 tablespoons beef fat, or 2 tablespoons peanut oil

8 good-quality pork sausages

24 scallions (not too thin), trimmed

scant 1 cup coarsely grated Cheddar cheese,

I wasn't brought up eating toad in the hole, so have no compunction about messing around with it. Beer in the batter really helps it to rise, but the most important thing is to get the tallow or oil in your roasting pan as hot as possible, as that's what really helps it to puff up.

Beat the eggs with electric beaters until they're foamy and thick. Add the flour, then the milk and beer alternately, beating on a low speed, until everything is incorporated and the batter is smooth. Add the mustard and season well. Cover and leave to sit for 30 minutes.

Preheat the oven to 400°F. Put half the beef fat or oil in a heavy roasting pan (the one I use measures 11½ x 9in) and melt it over medium heat. Add the sausages, turn them over in the fat, then roast for 10 minutes. Now add the scallions, turn both them and the sausages over in the fat, and roast for another 8 minutes. Remove the scallions and sausages from the roasting pan.

Increase the oven temperature to 425°F. Put the rest of the beef fat or oil in the pan and, when the oven has reached the new hotter temperature, heat it until smoking.

Carefully remove the pan from the oven. Return the scallions to it, pour the batter on top, then return the sausages. Bake for another 20 minutes.

Take the roasting pan out, sprinkle on the cheese, and return to the oven for a final 5 minutes. The batter should be puffed up and golden. Eat immediately.

SALSICCIA CON PATATE
E POMODORI AL FORNO

This is great both for dinner and as a weekend lunch. I don't know if it's particular to Sicily, though that's where I first ate it; it's such an obvious way to cook sausages and potatoes that I can't believe it's not done in other areas of Italy. You can use either waxy or russet potatoes; the russets will take a little less time to cook. (If you opt for small waxy potatoes, you don't need to peel them.) This calls for some peppery greens on the side.

Preheat the oven to 400°F.

Cut each sausage into 3 pieces. Heat 2 tablespoons of the olive oil in a wide, fairly shallow ovenproof pan, about 12in in diameter. Quickly brown the sausages all over: you just want to get a bit of color on the outside, not cook them through. Add the chili and fennel and cook for another minute.

Toss in the onions, potatoes, garlic, and peppers, and season. Add another couple of tablespoons of olive oil, unless a lot of fat has come out of the sausages (some exude a lot, others don't). Finish with most of the sausage pieces on top.

Cook in the oven for 20 minutes. Take the dish out of the oven and stir everything around. Put the tomatoes on top, season, sprinkle on the cheese, and drizzle on the remaining oil. Return to the oven and cook for a final 30–40 minutes, or until everything is golden and the potatoes are soft, gently stirring in whichever herb you want to use 10 minutes before the end of cooking time.

Serve in the dish in which it has been cooked.

SERVES 4

8 chunky, spicy, good-quality hot Italian sausages

⅓ cup extra virgin olive oil

¼ teaspoon crushed red pepper (you may want more if your sausages aren't that spicy)

¼ teaspoon fennel seeds, bashed a bit in a mortar

2 onions, thinly sliced

1lb potatoes, peeled and cut into slices about ⅛in thick

3 garlic cloves, finely sliced

1 red and 1 yellow bell peppers, halved, seeded, and sliced

sea salt flakes and freshly ground black pepper

1lb tomatoes, sliced

½ cup finely grated pecorino cheese,

2 tablespoons roughly chopped flat-leaf parsley leaves, or the leaves from 4 oregano sprigs

LAMB FILLET WITH HERB BUTTER, RADISHES & PEAS

Sticking frozen peas in the oven? As Nigella Lawson has shown us (she has a genius recipe for baked chicken thighs with leeks and peas in her book, At My Table)*, it works. The color of the peas and the radishes together is beautiful. The herb butter is the gilding of the lily here, so just leave it out if you don't want to make it and, instead, throw herbs in with the vegetables just before serving. Lamb loin is expensive, so this isn't a Wednesday night dish, more a Friday treat.*

Preheat the oven to 400°F.

To make the butter, just mash it with the herbs and seasoning, then slowly mash in the vermouth. You can put this in the refrigerator if you're making it in advance, otherwise it's fine to leave it at room temperature.

Put the peas into a 12in shallow casserole or sauté pan with the regular butter (not the herb butter), 1 tablespoon of the olive oil, the vermouth, and some seasoning. Cook in the oven for 25 minutes. After 10 minutes, toss the scallions and radishes in another 1 tablespoon of the oil and season. Stir the peas, then throw the scallions and radishes on top and return to the oven for their final 15 minutes.

Season the lamb with pepper and heat the last tablespoon of oil in an ovenproof frying pan over very high heat. Brown the fillets all over, then transfer them—in the pan—to the oven for 10 minutes. Take them out, cover with foil, and keep warm while letting the meat rest for 10 minutes.

Squeeze some lemon juice into the peas and radishes and add the mint leaves. Slice the lamb and serve it—with a pat of herb butter melting over the top—with the peas and radishes.

SERVES 4

FOR THE HERB BUTTER

5½ tablespoons unsalted butter, at room temperature

3 tablespoons chopped chervil or equal parts flat-leaf parsley leaves mixed with chives

sea salt flakes and freshly ground black pepper

1 tablespoon dry white vermouth

FOR THE LAMB AND VEGETABLES

1lb frozen peas

2 tablespoons unsalted butter

3 tablespoons extra virgin olive oil

⅔ cup dry white vermouth

10 thin scallions, trimmed

⅔lb radishes, halved lengthways

2 x 8oz boneless lamb loin pieces , trimmed

squeeze of lemon juice

handful of mint leaves, torn

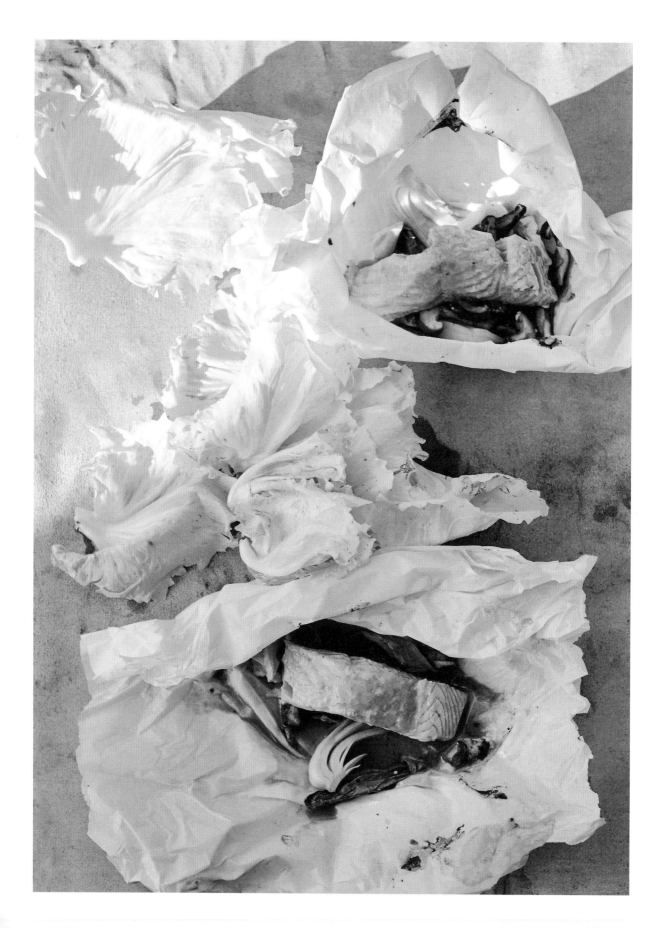

SALMON FILLETS WITH MISO, SHIITAKES & BOK CHOY

Serving dishes en papillote (*in parcels*) *means that juices are created around whatever you're cooking. The paper parcels don't have to be neat—so don't labor over them—and use foil if you'd prefer (it's easier, but doesn't look as good). As this is quite a sweet dish, I like some bitter greens with it, such as castelfranco, shown here, or frisée.*

Preheat the oven to 375°F.

Mix together the miso, honey, 2 tablespoons of the rice wine, the soy sauce, ginger, and sesame oil.

Put 4 rectangles of foil or parchment paper—each about 13½ x 9½in and of double thickness—on to 1 or 2 baking sheets (depending on the size of the sheets). Brush the center of each piece with peanut oil.

Divide the mushrooms and bok choy among the pieces of foil, placing them in the center (it will seem like a lot, but the vegetables really shrink as they cook). Sprinkle with the scallions.

Drizzle about 1 tablespoon of the miso mixture over the top of each heap of vegetables, then set a salmon fillet on top. Spread the rest of the miso mixture on top of each piece of fish (use all of it).

Pull the foil or paper up around the salmon, enclosing the vegetables and nipping the ends of each parcel, but let the top of each fish fillet remain exposed. Spoon the remaining rice wine into each parcel, dividing it evenly.

Bake for 12 minutes. Sprinkle the salmon with sesame seeds, if you're using them, and serve the fish in the parcels, with rice or noodles on the side.

SERVES 4

2 tablespoons white miso paste

2 tablespoons clear honey

7 tablespoons mirin, or dry vermouth or dry sherry

1 tablespoon light soy sauce

2 teaspoons peeled and finely grated fresh ginger

2 teaspoons toasted sesame oil

a little peanut oil

½lb shiitake mushrooms, trimmed and thinly sliced

2 heads of bok choy, sliced lengthwise

8 scallions, trimmed and roughly chopped

4¼lb salmon fillets, (not skinny fillets from the tail)

a few sesame seeds (optional)

rice or noodles, to serve

SERVES 4

FOR THE PORK
4 garlic cloves, finely grated
sea salt flakes
4 teaspoons caraway seeds
2 tablespoons extra virgin
olive oil
4 x ⅔lb thick pork chops, on
the bone

FOR THE VEGETABLES
generous 1lb cooked beets,
peeled and quartered
2 medium-sized tart apples,
halved, cored and each cut
into 12 wedges
2 onions, halved and sliced
about ½in thick
3 tablespoons extra virgin
olive oil
¼ cup cider vinegar
1½ tablespoons soft light
brown sugar
1 tablespoon Hungarian
sweet paprika
¼ teaspoon crushed red
pepper
sea salt flakes and freshly
ground black pepper

TO SERVE
sour cream
chopped dill (any thick stalks
discarded)

PORK CHOPS BAKED WITH BEETS, APPLES, CARAWAY & PAPRIKA

This is inspired by the flavors of Germany and Eastern Europe; it's a mixture of tastes and ingredients I love. Sour cream might seem a tad overindulgent (good chops have fat on them, so there's plenty of fat action going on), but even a small amount makes this dish sing, as it cuts the sweetness of the beets and apples.

Put the garlic into a mortar with the salt and caraway seeds and pound with the pestle. Add the olive oil, working it in until you have a rough paste. Put the pork chops in a bowl and add the mixture from the mortar, turning the chops over in it. Cover and marinate in the refrigerator for a while (at least 1 hour if possible, though longer is fine).

Preheat the oven to 375°F.

Put everything for the vegetables into a gratin dish or a roasting pan in which the beets and apples can lie in a single layer. Toss around with your hands and bake in the oven for 10 minutes.

Heat a frying or grill pan over high heat until very hot. Add the chops and color them on both sides, as well as on the fat (hold the chops on their sides, gripping them with tongs, so you can color the fat). Season with pepper and a little more salt.

Put the chops on top of the vegetables and pour over the cooking juices from the frying pan. Bake for a final 20 minutes; the meat should be cooked through but still tender.

Transfer to a warmed serving dish, or serve in the dish in which it was cooked. Spoon some sour cream scattered with dill over the vegetables, or just serve it on the side.

COD WITH CHORIZO, TOMATOES, OLIVES & SHERRY

It's funny to think that chorizo was once considered an exotic ingredient. We have taken the Spanish sausage so much to our hearts that it pops up everywhere (including where it has no business being). I love it, though, especially with fish and shellfish; its fatty smokiness is great with cod and mussels. This is a perfect all-in-one dish. Make sure to use the right kind of sherry (a too-sweet sherry will ruin this), though you could use fino instead of amontillado, if that's what you have.

Preheat the oven to 400°F. Put all the vegetables, the chorizo, and all the thyme into a roasting pan in which they can lie in a single layer. Season and add 2 tablespoons of the extra virgin olive oil (more oil will come out of the chorizo once it starts cooking). Toss everything around with your hands and roast in the oven for 30 minutes, turning the vegetables over a couple of times.

Now make the crust. Combine the breadcrumbs, garlic, lemon zest, herbs, and smoked paprika and season well. Pour in the melted butter and sherry and mix with a large fork or your fingers until combined. Brush the cod filets with the last tablespoon of oil, then cover them evenly with the crumbs, pressing down on them so they stick to the fish.

Mix the olives and sherry into the roasted vegetables and chorizo, then put the cod on top. Return to the oven and bake until the fish is cooked through: its flakes should be opaque, not translucent. This should take 15 minutes, but check for doneness and return the fish to the oven for no more than a couple of minutes if it needs a little longer. Serve with lemon wedges.

FOR THE COD AND CHORIZO

1lb baby potatoes, scrubbed and quartered

⅔lb cherry tomatoes on the vine

¼lb Spanish chorizo cooking sausages, sliced

leaves from 3 thyme sprigs, plus 3 whole thyme sprigs

sea salt flakes and freshly ground black pepper

3 tablespoons extra virgin olive oil

4 x 6oz thick cod fillets (not skinny fillets from the tail)

8-10 good-quality whole green olives

⅓ cup amontillado sherry

lemon wedges, to serve

FOR THE CRUST

1⅓ cups fresh white breadcrumbs

2 garlic cloves, crushed

finely grated zest of 1 small unwaxed lemon

1 tablespoon chopped flat-leaf parsley leaves

leaves from 2 thyme sprigs

¼ teaspoon smoked paprika

4 tablespoons unsalted butter, melted

½ tablespoon amontillado sherry

AT THE TABLE

I'm ticking off the items on my list scribbled, as usual, on the back of an envelope. The pears are lying in the pool of Marsala in which they've baked, and a glossy rubble of warm lentils with sausages on top has just come out of the oven. The table looks good. I've spent a lifetime collecting battered old cutlery and soft tablecloths and I love setting the table, even though I never do anything formal. There's just time to stick on a bit of lipstick—I rarely manage to change—before friends arrive. I feel a small thrill of excitement, but it's about the event rather than the food. Things happen at the table.

This is a book about getting dinner (or supper or whatever you call it) on the table every day, and about making food for friends. It's a cookbook. But a meal is always about more than the dishes served. Food isn't just physical sustenance, it's also about pleasure and about people. The "table" in the title of this book is just as important as the "oven." I wanted to write the book so that home cooks—and people who aren't confident in the kitchen—could get good food on to that table with relative ease, so a good time could be had by everyone, including the cook.

Having friends over is a performance of sorts. Casualness is now *de rigueur*, but even casualness requires a bit of thought. Despite what I do for a living, I don't often have big crowds of people around to eat. I tend to cook for friends who are staying, or small groups. I do uphold the kitchen table's role in our lives on a daily basis, though, which is a challenge when your children are teenagers. I won't relinquish our meals together and I know that if I let them slide for a few days we are all less happy. Sitting at the table is where we look at each other. The table makes it impossible not to. Then we talk, and if the food is good we're happy. We also, it's true, argue. But we communicate and, in a time when everything can be texted or emailed or sent on WhatsApp, that's important. The table is under threat. We eat alone more, on the sofa, standing up in the kitchen, at our computers, on the go. We try to squash eating into busy lives.

Not all cultures sit around a table to eat (estimates suggest that about a quarter of the world's population eat around a mat) and we haven't always done it in the West either. I'm not going to pretend that meals taken at a table are always and everywhere happy. They've served as a very conservative force (think of that Norman Rockwell Thanksgiving painting where everyone is relentlessly smiling). The 1950s American educational film *A Date with Your Family*—you can watch it online—now looks shocking in its emphasis on the roles assigned for the evening meal. The mother and daughter change their clothes because, the narrator tells us, "the women of this family seem to feel that they owe it to the men of the family to look relaxed, rested, and attractive," later adding, "the table is no place for discontent." It is, in fact, often a place of discontent. Many of the most memorable scenes in movies are about relationships collapsing at the table; in the Danish film, *Festen*, an entire extended family implodes, and in *American Beauty* the marriage between Lester and Carolyn Burnham bites the dust as the combatants fight across a table. A platter of asparagus ends up being thrown at the wall, the etiquette of the table literally smashed. If there are fault lines—in friendships, in marriages, in a family—the table is where they will be most evident.

But the table is, generally, a place where good things happen, or at least we hope they will. In 18th-century Dutch, a good friend is called a "table friend." When food is scarce—I'm particularly thinking of the meals that Russians put together when the country was part of the Soviet Union and it was hard to get hold of much—people try to create a feast that can be served at the table, even if it's just *salade Olivier* made with canned vegetables and industrial mayonnaise, pickled cabbage, buckwheat, and vodka.

In the last eighteen months—during the writing of this book—I've had more large groups of people over to eat than I've had in years and have been strongly reminded of what magical things can happen over a table. The American writer Adam Gopnik has said, "The test of a meal is the talk that it makes." It's better if the food is good, of course—if you're bothering to have people over you want them to experience pleasure, that is your gift to them—but it can be good in an ordinary way. Things have changed. As a child in the 1970s, I used to pore over the cooking pages in my mum's magazines, mentally noting what I would eventually need to pull off a bit of entertaining when I grew up (basically a chignon and a hostess trolley). Then, in the 1980s —when I started cooking for friends in earnest—I served up ridiculously complicated *nouvelle cuisine* meals that took days to prepare. But once molecular gastronomy came along, we all stopped trying to be chefs in our homes (thank God), because none of us had the equipment.

After a particular lovely lunch one Sunday (I served the chicken with orzo on page 175), my eldest child simply said: "Let's do this more." We'd invited old neighbors—a big sprawling garrulous family—and disparate friends who had just moved to London. People got to know each other simply by passing salt and bread, chairs were rearranged as small groups formed, noise levels were high, many jokes had been told, and I hadn't even bothered to serve the dessert "nicely" (I brought the ice cream to accompany the baked fruit to the table in its plastic tub). The food had been good, but not difficult or spectacular; everything had been transformed by the heat of the oven. As I looked at the mess when everyone had gone, words formed in my head, words that rang even truer than Gopnik's: "Your reward for cooking is laughter," I thought.

THYME-ROAST LAMB CHOPS WITH TOMATOES, BLACK OLIVES, POTATOES & GOAT CHEESE

Not an all-in-one dish, as you have to brown the chops and then put them on top of the vegetables, but even in the short period they're in the oven at the same time, the juices from the lamb flavor the potatoes, bringing both components together. The chops will take 10–12 minutes, depending on your oven. Keep an eye on them the first time you make this dish and then you'll know how long to cook them the next time.

Put the chops in a dish with 2 tablespoons of the olive oil and half the thyme. Cover and leave to marinate for at least 1 hour, or in the refrigerator overnight.

When you're ready to cook, preheat the oven to 400°F.

Put the potatoes, along with the tomatoes and onion, into a large gratin dish or a shallow casserole (about 12in across is ideal) in which all the vegetables can lie in a single layer. Add the rest of the oil, some salt and pepper, and the rest of the thyme. Separate the cloves of garlic and add those, too (you don't need to peel them). Toss everything together and roast in the oven for 25 minutes. Add the olives and scatter the goat cheese over the top. Spoon on a little more oil. Return the dish to the oven for 10 minutes.

Heat a frying pan over a very high heat until really hot, season the chops, and sear them until browned, about 1½ minutes on each side.

Put the chops on top of the vegetables and roast for a final 10 minutes, by which time they should be cooked through, but remain a little rare. The vegetables should be tender and the goat cheese toasted on top.

SERVES 4

8 thick loin lamb chops

4 tablespoons extra virgin olive oil, plus a little more

leaves from 5 thyme sprigs, plus 3 whole thyme sprigs

1lb small waxy potatoes, scrubbed, halved or quartered, depending on size

¾lb cherry tomatoes

1 large red onion, cut into wedges

sea salt flakes and freshly ground black pepper

1 head of garlic

scant 1 cup good-quality black olives, pitted or not, as you prefer

5½oz goat cheese, broken into rough chunks

CREAMY GRATIN OF FINNAN HADDIE, TOMATOES & POTATOES

This recipe does take a bit of effort, because the potatoes have to be so thinly sliced (a mandolin will save you a lot of time). You need a metal or cast-iron gratin dish, something that conducts heat well, otherwise it's difficult to cook the potatoes to tenderness in the time given.

Preheat the oven to 400°F. Put a metal baking sheet in the oven to heat up.

Cut the fish into slices about 1½in thick.

Slice the tomatoes thinly. You don't need to save the juice, so leave whatever runs out on to the chopping board, as the slices shouldn't be too wet. Slice the potatoes thinly, too—you don't need to peel them, just scrub them well—using a mandolin if you have one. It's important that the slices are really wafer-thin or the potatoes won't cook through in the time given and you'll have to cook the gratin for longer, which means the fish will be overcooked.

Layer half the potatoes and half the tomatoes in a metal gratin dish about 12in in diameter, or an oval-shaped dish measuring 14½ x 9in, with a capacity of 2 quarts, seasoning and sprinkling on the thyme as you do so.

Heat the cream and garlic to a boil, then strain it into a bowl and stir in the mustard, to taste. Pour half of the cream mixture over the vegetables.

Lay the fish on the cream-soaked vegetables, then add the rest of the vegetables and pour over the remaining hot cream. Sprinkle both cheeses on top.

Bake in the oven—sliding it onto the hot baking sheet—for 45–50 minutes, or until the potatoes are tender. Remove from the oven and leave to settle for 10 minutes, then serve.

SERVES 4–6

1lb finnan haddie or hot-smoked salmon fillets, skinned

scant 1lb tomatoes

1½lbs waxy new potatoes, such as gold creamers

sea salt flakes and freshly ground black pepper

leaves from 6 thyme sprigs

generous 2 cups heavy cream

1 garlic clove, sliced

1–2 teaspoons English or Dijon mustard, to taste

⅔ cup grated extra-sharp aged Cheddar cheese

generous ⅓ cup grated Parmesan cheese

SEARED & ROASTED DUCK BREASTS WITH ASIAN-FLAVORED PLUMS

The best way to cook duck breasts—and they make a handsome dinner (a bit of a treat)—is to "sear-roast" them: the fat starts to melt in the pan on the stovetop, then the meat cooks in the oven. It produces much more consistent results than you get from cooking the duck solely on the stovetop. Perfect every time—these timings give you rare meat—and far less demanding than standing over a pan, continually turning the meat.

Preheat the oven to 375°F.

Put everything for the plums into a roasting pan or ovenproof dish in which the plums can lie in a single layer, seasoning well with salt and pepper. Bake for 15 minutes, then turn the plums over and return to the oven to bake until they have completely collapsed (ripe plums may only need 20 minutes; really hard fruits could take as long as 35 minutes). Mash the cooked plums with a fork and taste for seasoning, then leave to cool.

Increase the oven temperature to 400°F.

Heat a large ovenproof frying pan and, when it's very hot, put the duck breasts in, skin side down. Cook until the fat starts to run out and the skin is seared and golden (3–4 minutes). Turn the breasts over and quickly cook them on the other side until colored. Season all over. Put the pan into the oven and roast the duck for 7 minutes.

Cut into the underside of a duck breast to see how well it's done: you want them rare—but not raw—in the center (if you don't like them very rare, cook for a little longer until they are the way you like them). Return them to the oven if they're not quite ready, though I wouldn't suggest you roast them for more than 10 minutes in total. When they're done, cover and set aside to rest for about 7 minutes so the juices can "set."

Carve the duck into slices and serve with the room-temperature plums.

FOR THE PLUMS

1¼lbs plums, halved and pitted

2 tablespoons clear honey

2½ tablespoons light brown sugar

1½ tablespoons soy sauce

2 broad strips of orange zest, plus juice of ½ orange

½ teaspoon ground ginger

½ teaspoon five spice powder

1½ teaspoons crushed red pepper

2 garlic cloves, finely grated

sea salt flakes and freshly ground black pepper

FOR THE DUCK

4 duck breasts

PORK BELLY STRIPS WITH SCALLION SALAD & KOREAN DIPPING SAUCE

This is based on a Korean dish called samgyeopsal-gui. *You can get both the Korean pastes online (larg supermarkets now carry them, too) and they have a long shelf life.*

Preheat the oven to 350°F.

Dry the pork belly slices with paper towels—if they're damp they won't brown—then put into a roasting pan large enough for them to lie in a single layer. Brush with oil, season, and cook for about 90 minutes, turning the pork over twice during the cooking time and pouring off the excess fat. When they're ready, they should be meltingly tender and golden brown, but sometimes, depending on your oven, they will need a quick blast at 425°F, just until they turn a good color.

To make the dipping sauce, stir both the pastes together in a small bowl with the sesame oil, maple syrup or honey, and garlic. Set aside.

For the salad, stir the soy sauce and sugar together in a small salad bowl until the sugar has dissolved, then mix in the sesame oil and red pepper powder or crushed red pepper to make a dressing.

Soak the scallions in cold water for 5 minutes, then drain and dry. Halve them horizontally, then shred them lengthwise, so that you end up with very fine slices. Toss the soy-sauce dressing with the scallions and sprinkle the sesame seeds on top.

Serve the meat with the dipping sauce, the scallion salad, and crispy vegetables: raw carrot and cucumber sticks are good, as well as lettuce leaves (the crispness of iceberg works well here).

SERVES 4

FOR THE PORK AND SAUCE

2½lbs boneless 1-inch thick pork belly slices

a little peanut oil

sea salt flakes and freshly ground black pepper

3 tablespoons *doenjang* soy bean paste

2 tablespoons *gochujang* chili paste

2 tablespoons toasted sesame oil

2 tablespoons maple syrup or clear honey

2 garlic cloves, finely grated

carrot and cucumber sticks and crisp lettuce, to serve

FOR THE SALAD

3 tablespoons soy sauce

2 teaspoons light brown sugar

2 tablespoons toasted sesame oil

½ teaspoon *gochugaru* (Korean red pepper powder), or ½ teaspoon crushed red pepper

10 thin scallions, trimmed

1 teaspoon sesame seeds

LAMB CHOPS WITH SWEET POTATOES, PEPPERS & MOJO VERDE

Mojo verde *is Spanish for "green sauce" and comes from the Canary Islands. There's also a red version and hundreds of variations on each (some more spicy than others, some more citrusy). I love the green sauce with sweet potatoes, pork, meaty fish, and duck breasts.*

Put the lamb chops in a dish—or in a plastic food storage bag—with the cumin, some seasoning, and half the olive oil. Cover (or seal) and put in the refrigerator while you get on with everything else.

Preheat the oven to 375°F.

Put the sweet potatoes, onions, and peppers into a roasting pan in which they can lie more or less in a single layer. Season and add the remaining oil. Toss the vegetables and roast for 30 minutes, turning them once during that time.

To make the *mojo verde*, put everything in a food processor and blitz. (You will have to push the ingredients down the sides of the bowl a couple of times.) Taste for seasoning.

Heat a frying pan over high heat until really hot, then sear the chops until browned, about 1½ minutes on each side.

Take the roasting pan out of the oven and put the chops on top of the vegetables. Return to the oven and cook for a final 10 minutes, by which time the chops should be cooked through, but remain a little rare.

Serve the lamb chops and vegetables with the *mojo verde*.

SERVES 4

FOR THE LAMB AND VEGETABLES

8 thick loin lamb chops

1 teaspoon ground cumin

sea salt flakes and freshly ground black pepper

5 tablespoons extra virgin olive oil

1½lbs sweet potatoes, peeled, or scrubbed and unpeeled, as you prefer, cut into chunks

2 medium onions, cut into slim wedges

2 red bell peppers, halved, seeded, and cut into broad strips

FOR THE MOJO VERDE

3 garlic cloves, chopped

1 green bell pepper, halved, seeded, and chopped

5 tablespoons extra virgin olive oil

2 tablespoons white wine vinegar

1 teaspoon ground cumin

8 cups cilantro leaves

SERVES 4

FOR THE BUTTER

7 tablespoons unsalted
butter, at room temperature

4 scallions, trimmed and
finely chopped

½in fresh ginger, peeled and
finely grated

2 tablespoons soy sauce

FOR THE STEAK

peanut oil, or beef fat, if you
have it

4 x ½lb sirloin steaks, each
about 1¼in thick

sea salt flakes and freshly
ground black pepper

STEAK WITH SOY-GINGER BUTTER

*This method for cooking steak—searing over a very high heat, then
transferring to the oven—might seem unorthodox, but I learned
it from chef Neil Rankin, who knows a thing or two about meat
cookery. It works every time. He doesn't even rest the steaks after
cooking them like this (the juices don't run out when you cut into the
meat). If you have cast-iron frying pans that can go in the oven, use
those, so you won't have to transfer the steaks to a roasting pan or
baking sheet. This makes more butter than you need, but it's hard to
work with smaller quantities: try it on fish or corn on the cob. I even
like it on toast (deliciously umami).*

Mash the butter with the scallions, ginger, and soy sauce, gradually working in
the soy sauce until amalgamated. You can leave this at room temperature or put it
in the refrigerator. Some people like to chill the butter a little, then shape it into
a log and wrap it in greaseproof paper, so you can cut it into rounds. (I hate how
long it takes the cold butter to melt, so I prefer it at room temperature.)

Preheat the oven to 300°F. Put in an empty roasting pan or metal baking sheet
to heat up, large enough to hold all the steaks.

Heat 1 large frying pan (or 2 smaller ones)—cast iron, if possible—for
7–10 minutes. Add a tiny bit of oil or beef fat. Once it smokes, it is ready.

Put the steaks into the pan. First hold the fat of each of them against the bottom
of the pan to render it a little and add color—you need to grip each steak with
tongs as you do this—then lay the steaks flat and press down with your tongs.
Season and flip the steaks frequently, moving them round the pan and making
sure you can hear them sizzle. If the pan gets too hot—and the steak is becoming
too dark—reduce the heat (you want a good color, but not burned meat).

Once the surfaces are well colored—this should take about 4 minutes—transfer
the steaks to the hot roasting pan or baking sheet in the oven. Finish cooking the
steaks in the oven: 2 minutes for rare, 5 minutes for medium-rare.

Serve the steaks with a pat of the soy-ginger butter melting over the top.

MY FAVORITE
INGREDIENT
CHICKEN THIGHS
FOREVER

CHICKEN WITH FETA CHEESE, DILL, LEMON & HARISSA YOGURT

SERVES 4

1lb small waxy potatoes, scrubbed and quartered

2 red onions, halved and cut into wedges

1 head of garlic, cloves separated but not peeled

3 tablespoons extra virgin olive oil

sea salt flakes and freshly ground black pepper

8 good-sized skin-on, bone-in chicken thighs, excess skin neatly trimmed

finely grated zest of 1 unwaxed lemon, plus juice of ½ lemon

½–⅔ cup feta cheese, crumbled

⅔ cup dill leaves, torn

1 cup Greek yogurt

1 tablespoon harissa

All the dishes in this chapter are made with chicken thighs, because I unashamedly love them. They're succulent—so much better than breasts, which can dry out, in fact it's hard to overcook chicken thighs—they all cook at the same time (and quickly), and there's no carving. If you like a mixture of thighs and drumsticks, all the recipes on the pages that follow will work with those, too, just replace half the thighs in any dish with drumsticks. Lots of the relishes on pages 206–207 would work with roast chicken thighs, just cook the meat as below, leaving out the feta cheese, dill, and lemon, and serve it with a relish instead.

Preheat the oven to 400°F.

Put the potatoes, onions, garlic cloves, 2 tablespoons of the oil, salt, and pepper into a 12in wide shallow casserole or ovenproof sauté pan. Toss everything around with your hands. Put the chicken thighs on top, skin side up. Brush the remaining oil on the chicken and season it.

Roast for 40–45 minutes, or until the chicken is golden and the potatoes are tender when pierced with a sharp knife.

Squeeze the lemon juice over, then scatter on the zest, feta, and dill.

Put the yogurt into a bowl and spoon the harissa on top. Serve the chicken with the harissa yogurt on the side.

CHICKEN WITH MISO, SWEET POTATOES & SCALLIONS

This is my "Lost in Translation" dish. I don't know that much about Japanese food, but you start with any cuisine by feeling your way, then gradually you fall for its flavors. I have come to love miso and the big umami punch it delivers, especially when used with sweet ingredients.

Preheat the oven to 400°F.

Put the chicken thighs or joints into a big roasting pan with the sweet potato wedges (they should be able to lie—more or less—in a single layer).

In a small bowl, mix everything else together, except the scallions and sesame seeds. Pour this over the chicken and sweet potatoes, turning everything over so the ingredients get well coated. Finish with the chicken skin side up.

Roast for 45 minutes, basting every so often and turning the sweet potato wedges over.

Stir the ingredients for the final basting together in another small bowl.

About 15 minutes before the end of cooking time, take the pan out of the oven, add the scallions, and pour the final basting mixture over everything. Return to the oven. The scallions should become soft and slightly charred.

Transfer the chicken and vegetables to a warmed platter and sprinkle with the sesame seeds. Serve immediately, with stir-fried green vegetables.

SERVES 4–6

FOR THE CHICKEN

8 good-sized skin-on, bone-in chicken thighs, excess skin neatly trimmed

1½lbs sweet potatoes, scrubbed and cut into wedges

2½ tablespoons white miso paste

1½ tablespoons clear honey

2 tablespoons sake, or dry sherry

1 tablespoon dark soy sauce

1in fresh ginger, peeled and finely grated

3 garlic cloves, finely grated

1 red Fresno chili, halved and finely chopped (use the seeds)

12–18 scallions, trimmed

3 teaspoons black or toasted white sesame seeds (or a mixture of both)

stir-fried green vegetables, to serve

FOR THE FINAL BASTING

1 tablespoon white miso paste

1 tablespoon clear honey

½ tablespoon dark soy sauce

½ tablespoon sake, or dry sherry

CHICKEN WITH PLUMS, HONEY & POMEGRANATES

Try to find crimson-fleshed plums, as they look stunning, and use walnuts instead of pistachios in the relish for a change (walnuts lend a slightly sweet-bitter, woody flavor). Couscous or bulgur wheat and a bowl of Greek yogurt are good on the side. This is cooked at a slightly lower temperature than the other chicken thigh recipes, because honey can burn if the heat is too high. If the skin is getting very dark, cover the roasting pan with foil.

Preheat the oven to 375°F.

Put the chicken thighs into a 12in ovenproof dish or shallow casserole in which they can all lie in a single layer. Add the sumac, ground coriander, half the garlic, and all the olive oil, and season. Turn everything over with your hands to make sure it's coated, then cover and marinate in the refrigerator for 1 hour, if you have the time. Mix the onions with the chicken and the marinade, then arrange the thighs so they are skin side up. Dot half the plums among the chicken.

In a small bowl, stir the honey and pomegranate molasses together with the cayenne pepper, cumin, orange zest, and the remaining garlic. Spoon half of this over the chicken and plums. Sprinkle half the sugar on the plums and season them, then pour the orange juice around.

Roast for 25 minutes, then spoon the rest of the honey and pomegranate molasses over the chicken skin. Add the remaining plums and sprinkle them with the remaining sugar. Return to the oven to cook for a final 20 minutes.

For the relish, bash the nuts in a mortar with the garlic and some salt. Add the cilantro and bash a bit more to break it all down a bit, not grind it into a paste, then stir in the olive oil and lemon juice. Season to taste, then spoon it over the chicken and scatter with pomegranate seeds.

SERVES 4

FOR THE CHICKEN

8 good-sized, skin-on bone-in chicken thighs, excess skin neatly trimmed

2 teaspoons ground sumac

1 teaspoon ground coriander

4 garlic cloves, finely grated

3 tablespoons extra virgin olive oil

sea salt flakes and freshly ground black pepper

2 red onions, cut into fine crescent moon-shaped slices

8 plums (preferably crimson-fleshed and firm), halved and pitted

¼ cup clear honey

3 tablespoons pomegranate molasses

½ teaspoon cayenne pepper

1½ teaspoons ground cumin

finely grated zest of ½ orange

4 teaspoons soft light brown sugar

¼ cup orange juice

3 tablespoons pomegranate seeds

FOR THE PISTACHIO RELISH

2½ tablespoons shelled unsalted pistachio nuts, chopped

1 garlic clove, finely chopped

3 tablespoons chopped cilantro leaves

1 tablespoon extra virgin olive oil

lemon juice, to taste

CHICKEN WITH LEMON, CAPERS & THYME

This is simplicity itself, but you still have to take care: if you put the lemon slices on top from the start they'll burn, so keep them tucked away under the chicken and vegetables until you get near the end of cooking time. Green or black olives could also be added about five minutes before the end. This dish would be lovely with Baked Peppers Stuffed with Goat Cheese, Ricotta & Basil (see page 77); you can cook them in the oven at the same time.

Preheat the oven to 400°F.

Put the potatoes into a shallow casserole dish 12in across, or a roasting pan in which all the vegetables can lie in a single layer. Add the onions, garlic cloves, and thyme. Finely grate the zest of 1 lemon over this and squeeze on the juice of half of it. Cut the other lemon into fine slices (flick out any seeds you see).

Add 2 tablespoons of the extra virgin olive oil to the vegetables and season them. Toss the lemon slices in and turn everything over with your hands.

Put the chicken thighs on top, skin side up, and brush them with the remaining olive oil. Season them, too. Make sure no lemon slices are sticking out, as they will burn quickly; they should be tucked under the chicken.

Roast in the oven for 30 minutes. Retrieve some of the lemon slices and put them on top of the chicken, so they can turn golden in the last bit of cooking time. Scatter the capers over and return to the oven for a final 10 minutes. Serve immediately.

SERVES 4

1¼lbs small waxy potatoes, scrubbed and cut into 1in chunks

2 onions, cut into crescent moon-shaped wedges

1 head of garlic, cloves separated but not peeled

10 thyme sprigs

2 unwaxed lemons

3 tablespoons extra virgin olive oil

sea salt flakes and freshly ground black pepper

8 good-sized skin-on bone-in chicken thighs, excess skin neatly trimmed

3 tablespoons capers, drained, rinsed, and patted dry

CHICKEN WITH HOT ITALIAN SAUSAGES & RED BELL PEPPERS

Chicken thighs can vary a lot in size. For this to feed eight, you need big pieces; it will feed fewer if the thighs are on the small side. Try to find good-quality sweet Italian sausages, the type that are flavored with chili or fennel are good for this.

Preheat the oven to 375°F.

Heat half the olive oil in a big, shallow casserole dish in which the thighs can lie in a single layer, or use a heavy roasting pan that can go on the stovetop and in the oven. Quickly brown the chicken on both sides—you don't want to cook it through, just get some color on it—then remove from the pan. Do the same with the sausages, coloring them all over.

Cut the sausages on the diagonal into pieces. Halve and deseed the peppers and cut each half into 4 pieces lengthwise.

Toss the peppers and onions into the casserole or roasting pan with the crushed red pepper, garlic, seasoning, the rest of the oil, the sherry vinegar, rosemary, and sausages. Turn everything over with your hands. Put the chicken, skin side up, on top of this.

Bake in the oven for 40–45 minutes, turning the vegetables over a couple of times. The chicken should be cooked through. Serve either with little potatoes that you've roasted in olive oil (*see* pages 107–109), or with mashed potatoes, or rice pilaf (mashed potatoes or rice pilaf scented and colored with saffron would be lovely with this).

SERVES 6–8

3 tablespoons extra virgin olive oil

8 good-sized skin-on. bone-in chicken thighs, excess skin neatly trimmed

1lb good-quality sweet Italian sausages

3 red bell peppers

2 red onions, halved and cut into crescent moon-shaped slices

1 teaspoon crushed red pepper

8 garlic cloves, finely grated

sea salt flakes and freshly ground black pepper

2 tablespoons sherry vinegar

leaves from 1 rosemary sprig, plus 3 whole rosemary sprigs

olive oil-roasted potatoes, mashed potatoes, or rice pilaf, to serve

CHICKEN WITH DIJON MUSTARD, CRÈME FRAÎCHE & VERMOUTH

This recipe shows precisely how roasting—with a little liquid underneath the chicken—can produce a better dish than sautéing. Here, a lovely sauce is created below the chicken as it cooks, while its skin ends up with a golden "crust" on top. I've adapted the dish from one in Molly Stevens' All About Roasting. *If you're into roasting, it's a must-have book.*

Preheat the oven to 400°F.

Put the chicken thighs into a heavy roasting pan in which they can lie in a single layer, sitting snugly together with not much room around them, or into a 12in shallow casserole.

In a small bowl, mix the mustard with the olive oil and spread this all over the skin of the chicken. Season with pepper (there's a lot of salt in the Dijon mustard). Mix the garlic with the crème fraîche and dollop it on top of the chicken (it doesn't have to be neat, as it will melt and run off the chicken once it goes into the oven). Pour in about two-thirds of the vermouth at the sides so it runs underneath the chicken.

Cook for 40 minutes, adding the rest of the vermouth halfway through.

Put the chicken onto a warmed plate and cover it with foil and a couple of tea towels to keep it warm.

Quickly bring the juices in the roasting pan or casserole to the boil and reduce them a little so they thicken. Add the parsley and lemon juice and whisk in the butter, bit by bit. Return the chicken to the sauce, then serve.

SERVES 4

8 good-sized skin-on, bone-in chicken thighs, excess skin neatly trimmed

¼ cup Dijon mustard

1 tablespoon extra virgin olive oil

freshly ground black pepper

½ garlic clove, finely grated

⅓ cup crème fraîche

⅔ cup dry white vermouth

2 tablespoons very finely chopped flat-leaf parsley leaves

squeeze of lemon juice

1 tablespoon cold unsalted butter, chopped

CHICKEN WITH TORN SOURDOUGH, SHERRY, RAISINS & BITTER GREENS

There's a lot going on here, though it's a very simple dish. The sourdough pieces end up crunchy with a moist, slightly boozy, garlic-infused underside. There is sweetness from the sherry and raisins, bitterness from the greens, and saltiness from the bacon. It's all about contrast. Use watercress—just arrange small fistfuls among the cooked chicken—if you aren't keen on bitter greens, and up the red pepper if you want more heat.

Preheat the oven to 400°F.

Put the bread, potatoes, onion, thyme, crushed red pepper, and garlic cloves into a large roasting pan. Cut the pancetta or bacon into ½in chunks and add them to the pan with the chicken. Pour on the sherry vinegar, ¼ cup of the sherry, and 4 tablespoons olive oil. Season and toss everything around with your hands, finishing with the chicken skin side up. Make sure the bread isn't too exposed, or lying at the edges, or it will burn.

Roast for 25 minutes—tossing the ingredients around once, but making sure the chicken is still skin side up—then add another ¼ cup sherry.

Mix the scallions in a bowl with the remaining olive oil and add them to the pan, too, laying them on top of the vegetables. Return to the oven and roast for a final 15 minutes.

Pour the remaining sherry into a small saucepan with the raisins and bring to just under a boil. Let sit, then add them to the roasting pan 5 minutes before the end of the cooking time.

Transfer everything to a large warmed platter or broad, shallow serving dish (unless you're happy to take the roasting pan to the table) and mix in whichever of the greens you want to use (or just serve them on the side). Throw on the pine nuts and serve.

SERVES 4

1½ cups sourdough bread, torn into pieces roughly 2in square

1lb small waxy potatoes, scrubbed and cut into chunks

1 large onion, cut into wedges

6 thyme sprigs

2 teaspoons crushed red pepper

1 head of garlic, cloves separated but not peeled

⅓lb pancetta or slab bacon, in 1 piece

8 good-sized skin-on, bone-in chicken thighs, excess skin neatly trimmed

2 tablespoons sherry vinegar

1 cup amontillado sherry

5 tablespoons extra virgin olive oil

sea salt flakes and freshly ground black pepper

10 thin scallions, trimmed

⅓ cup raisins

¼lb bitter salad greens (such as radicchio, Belgian endive, frisée, dandelion or treviso)

3 tablespoons toasted pine nuts

CHICKEN & CAULIFLOWER
WITH 'NDUJA

SERVES 4

8 good-sized skin-on, bone-in chicken thighs, excess skin neatly trimmed

1 x 1lb head cauliflower, broken into florets

1lb baby waxy potatoes, scrubbed, then halved or quartered, depending on size

2¾oz 'nduja, broken into nuggets

6 thyme sprigs

3 tablespoons olive oil

sea salt flakes and freshly ground black pepper

green salad, or bitter greens, to serve

The work here is done in about eight minutes flat and the end result is totally moreish. I cook this a lot. You need to toss the elements around a few times during the cooking—to make sure the cauliflower colors all over—but that's it. Add red onion wedges, too, if you want. 'Nduja is a spicy, spreadable Calabrian sausage; get it online or from good Italian delis.

Preheat the oven to 400°F.

Put all the ingredients in a roasting pan or a broad, shallow casserole about 12in across, season, and toss around with your hands. The chicken should end up skin-side up. Make sure the nuggets of 'nduja aren't lying on top, or they'll burn.

Roast for 40–45 minutes, turning everything over about 3 times during the cooking. The 'nduja partly melts and you need to ensure it gets well mixed in.

Towards the end of the cooking time, it's good to spoon the bits of 'nduja over the chicken, as it gives it a lovely color. The potatoes should be tender when pierced with a sharp knife and the chicken cooked through. Serve with a green salad or bitter greens.

CHICKEN WITH PRUNES, POTATOES, CAULIFLOWER & HARISSA

The flavors of a tagine without the fuss. This dish is quite sweet, because of the prunes, so it does need the preserved lemon to cut through that. If you don't like prunes (I know they divide people), use dried apricots or pitted dates instead.

Preheat the oven to 400°F.

In a bowl, mix together the harissa, spices, garlic, sugar, salt and pepper, and olive oil.

Cut the potatoes—there's no need to peel them—into very thin (¹⁄₁₆in) slices and put them into a shallow 12in casserole with the onions. Add the cauliflower and prunes. Take one-third of the harissa mixture and toss it with the vegetables. Add the chicken stock and place over medium heat until the mixture is simmering.

Remove the flesh from the preserved lemons—keep the rind for scattering on top—chop it, then add it to the rest of the harissa mixture, along with the brine from the jar. Mix the chicken thighs with this mixture, rubbing it all over. Set the chicken on top of the simmering vegetables, skin side up. Season the chicken and put the dish into the oven.

Cook for 45 minutes, taking the dish out and scooping the cooking juices up over the chicken a couple of times. You should end up with dark, golden chicken and tender vegetables.

Cut the preserved lemon rind into shreds and throw it over the chicken along with the cilantro. This is good with a nut relish (*see* page 50), made with pistachios or walnuts. If you want to serve a grain on the side, see pages 150–151 for some suggestions. A bowl of Greek yogurt—you can grate some garlic into it or leave it as it is—is excellent, though.

SERVES 4

2½ tablespoons harissa

1 teaspoon ground turmeric

1 teaspoon ground ginger

½ teaspoon ground cinnamon

1 teaspoon ground cumin

4 garlic cloves, finely grated

1 tablespoon light brown sugar

sea salt flakes and freshly ground black pepper

2 tablespoons extra virgin olive oil

1lb small waxy potatoes, scrubbed

2 onions, sliced

¾lb cauliflower florets

about 12 moist prunes (more is fine)

1¼ cups chicken stock

2 preserved lemons, plus 1½ tablespoons brine from the jar

8 good-sized skin-on. bone-in chicken thighs, excess skin neatly trimmed

3 tablespoons roughly chopped cilantro leaves

Pistachio Relish, to serve (optional, see page 50)

Greek yogurt, to serve

ASPARAGUS
TO ZUCCHINI

SPRING & SUMMER
VEGETABLES

CUMIN-ROASTED STRING BEANS & TOMATOES WITH TAHINI & CILANTRO

If you've never roasted string beans, you've been missing out. They stay a little crisp, wrinkle ever so slightly, and have a more intense flavor than beans cooked in (or over) water. You need to pay attention to timings, though. The beans can turn from perfect to overdone quite suddenly.

Preheat the oven to 400°F.

Put the tomatoes into a roasting pan or on a baking sheet that has a lip all the way around. There needs to be room to add the beans later. Toss the tomatoes with 1 tablespoon of the oil and season them well. Roast in the oven for 10 minutes.

Toss the string beans in a bowl with the remaining 1 tablespoon of oil and the cumin seeds. Scatter the beans on top and around the tomatoes. Return to the oven for a final 10 minutes. At the end of the roasting time, the tomatoes should be completely soft and the beans slightly charred.

To make the dressing, mix all the ingredients together in a bowl and season well. The tahini will "seize" and thicken when you add the lemon juice, but don't worry, it will break down again when you add the water and beat hard with a wooden spoon. Tahini varies in thickness, so you might need more water than I've suggested here to achieve a dressing as thick as cream.

Spoon the dressing onto a plate, place the vegetables on top, and scatter with the sesame seeds and cilantro. You can serve this at room temperature, though I prefer it slightly warm.

SERVES 6 AS A SIDE DISH

FOR THE VEGETABLES

1lb 2oz cherry tomatoes, mixed colors if possible

2 tablespoons extra virgin olive oil

sea salt flakes and freshly ground black pepper

1lb 2oz string beans, stem ends removed

1½ teaspoons cumin seeds

2 teaspoons sesame seeds

2 tablespoons roughly chopped cilantro leaves

FOR THE TAHINI DRESSING

¼ cup tahini

juice of ½ lemon

5 tablespoons water, plus more if needed

2 garlic cloves, finely grated

4 tablespoons extra virgin olive oil

1½ teaspoons clear honey

WHOLE EGGPLANTS WITH SAFFRON, BLACK CARDAMOM & DATE BUTTER

SERVES 6 AS A SIDE DISH

FOR THE BUTTER

good pinch of saffron threads

6 black cardamom pods

4 tablespoons unsalted butter, at room temperature

4 Medjool dates, pitted and chopped

2 garlic cloves, crushed

¼ teaspoon cayenne pepper, or to taste

generous pinch of ground ginger, or to taste

sea salt flakes, to taste

FOR THE EGGPLANTS

6¾lb globe eggplants

a little extra virgin olive oil

black sesame seeds, to serve

plain yogurt, to serve

It seems odd to pair eggplants with butter—we more often think of them being cooked with oil—but ghee is used with them in Indian cooking, so why not? Butter can really melt into cooked eggplant; in fact, I think the flesh soaks it up better than oil. I use black cardamom—which has a smoky, slightly meaty flavor—in the butter here, but you can use green cardamom, though the results are quite different. With soft bread—naan is best—and yogurt flavored with cilantro and garlic, this makes a meal.

Preheat the oven to 400°F.

For the butter, put the saffron into a small bowl or cup and add ½ tablespoon boiling water. Stir, then leave to cool. Break the cardamom pods open and remove the seeds. Grind them as well as you can with a mortar and pestle.

Put the butter into a bowl, add the saffron and cardamom, and stir and mash to combine well. Add the dates, garlic, cayenne, and ginger, and season well with salt. Stir and mash to combine again, then taste: you may want more cayenne or ginger, but these spices shouldn't overwhelm the cardamom. Shape the butter into a log and wrap it in parchment paper, or just transfer it to a bowl and cover it. Either way, it needs to go into the refrigerator (because of the dates, this is better a little chilled).

Put the eggplants in a roasting pan and brush lightly with some of the oil. Pierce each one a few times with the tines of a fork. Roast for 40–45 minutes, or until the eggplants are completely soft and look a bit deflated.

Slit the eggplants down the middle. Add pats of the spiced date butter and allow them to melt. Sprinkle on sesame seeds, and serve with a bowl of yogurt.

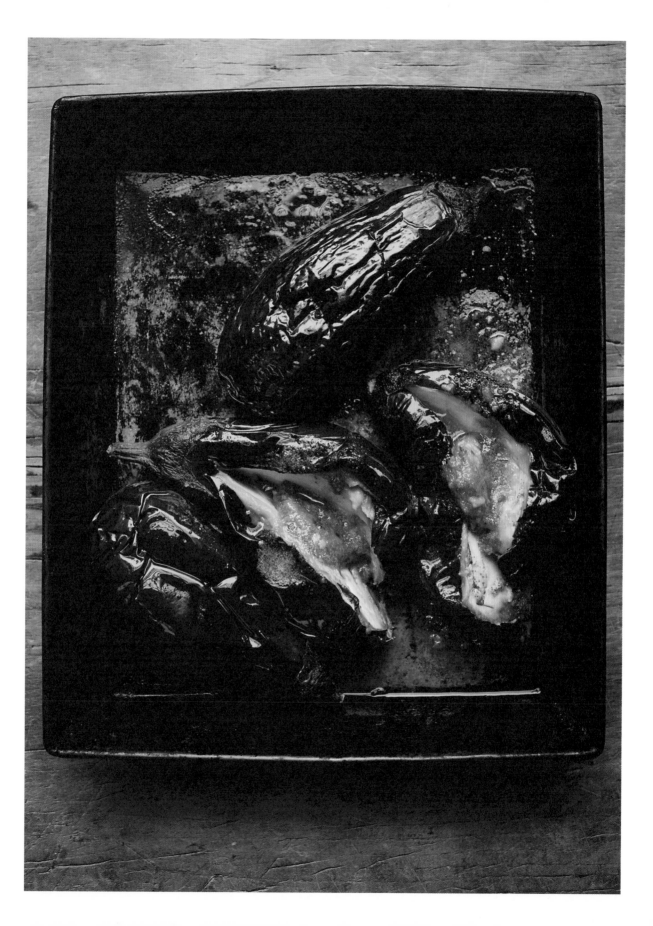

GREEK ZUCCHINI, POLENTA, FETA CHEESE & DILL "PIE"

This is based on a Greek dish that sounded very promising, but I had to cook it many times before I got a "set" that was soft, rather than like an oven-baked frittata. It's definitely a main course dish. I often eat it just with salad.

Preheat the oven to 400°F.

Put the zucchini into a large roasting pan in which they can lie—more or less—in a single layer. Toss them with 2 tablespoons of the olive oil and season. Roast for 10 minutes, then add the scallions and trickle the remaining 1 tablespoon of oil over them. Return to the oven and roast for another 10–15 minutes. By this time, the zucchini should be tender when pierced with a sharp knife, and the scallions slightly charred.

Reduce the oven temperature to 350°F.

In a large bowl, mix together all the other ingredients and season well. Spoon the vegetables into a gratin dish; mine measures 10½ x 8 x 2in and has a capacity of 1 quart. A cast-iron or tin-lined copper dish is best, because the metals conduct heat well. Pour the batter over the vegetables and bake in the oven for 15–20 minutes, or until just set, golden, and slightly souffléd. Serve hot or warm, scattered with dill.

SERVES 4, OR 6–8 AS
A SIDE DISH

2¼lbs zucchini, cut into
¾in thick slices

3 tablespoons extra virgin
olive oil

sea salt flakes and freshly
ground black pepper

8 thin scallions, trimmed

5 large eggs, lightly beaten

⅔ cup Greek yogurt

scant ¼ cup instant polenta

scant 1 cup crumbled feta
cheese

1 cup finely grated kefalotyri
or pecorino cheese

¼ cup chopped dill leaves,
any thick stalks discarded,
plus more to serve

3 garlic cloves, finely grated

CHILI-ROASTED TOMATOES WITH FETA CHEESE, YOGURT, DILL, MINT & PISTACHIOS

SERVES 4 AS A SIDE DISH,
OR AS PART OF A SPREAD
OF DISHES

1⅔lbs plum tomatoes,
halved lengthwise

4 tablespoons extra virgin
olive oil

3 teaspoons crushed red
pepper

2 teaspoons fennel seeds

sea salt flakes and freshly
ground black pepper

4 teaspoons clear honey

1 cup Greek yogurt, or more,
depending on the size of
your serving plate

1 cup crumbled feta cheese

1 garlic clove, finely grated

⅓ cup dill, chopped, any
thick stalks removed

scant 1 cup mint leaves

1 tablespoon chopped
shelled unsalted pistachio
nuts

Cooking is often about balance and contrast, and I particularly like dishes where the contrast is extreme. Hot, spicy tomatoes with cold, sharp yogurt is especially hard to resist. You can change the herbs here: dill, mint, chervil, and cilantro all work. Using chopped walnuts instead of pistachios makes quite a difference, too. It's definitely time to get out your favorite extra virgin olive oil. A Ligurian oil makes this buttery, a Greek oil a bit more robust: your choice will really change the character of the dish.

Preheat the oven to 400°F.

Put all the tomatoes into a roasting pan in which they can lie in a single layer; if they are too close to each other, they will steam instead of roasting. Spoon 3 tablespoons of the oil over them, then turn them over with your hands so they get well coated. Leave them cut sides up.

Put the crushed red pepper and fennel seeds into a mortar and bash them. You won't break the fennel seeds down, but you'll crush them a bit. Sprinkle these over the tomatoes and season. Mix the honey with the remaining olive oil and spoon a little over each tomato.

Cook for 30 minutes. Keep an eye on them; you may find they need a little longer, but don't overcook them. They get to a point when they completely collapse and—even though they're delicious at this stage—they've lost all their shape and you don't want that here.

Stir the yogurt, feta, and garlic together and season. Put the yogurt mixture on a serving plate and pile the roast tomatoes on top. Sprinkle the herbs and pistachios all over the dish and serve.

ROASTED RADISHES WITH HONEY, MINT & PRESERVED LEMON

SERVES 4 AS A SIDE DISH

1lb 2oz radishes, with green leaves attached

1 tablespoon extra virgin olive oil

1 tablespoon white balsamic vinegar

1 preserved lemon, flesh discarded, rind cut into shreds, plus 2 tablespoons brine from the jar, plus more if needed

1 tablespoon unsalted butter

sea salt flakes and freshly ground black pepper

1½ tablespoons clear honey

leaves from 6 mint sprigs, torn

I used to think that roasting radishes was done just for the sake of creating something different. I couldn't see how their peppery crunch could be improved upon. But cooked radishes are just different. They retain a little of their heat—though it's muted— and they don't soften completely. They're very good with butter and a drop of lemon juice or vinegar. You need perfect radishes for this dish, crispily fresh with plenty of perky leaves.

Preheat the oven to 400°F.

Wash the radishes well and remove their leaves (keep them fresh: you can wrap them in damp paper towels and put them in the refrigerator).

Halve the radishes lengthwise. Put them in a roasting pan with the olive oil, white balsamic, half the preserved lemon brine, and all the butter. Season. Roast for 7 minutes.

Add the remaining tablespoon of brine and the honey. Shake the pan around and return to the oven for a final 10 minutes.

Transfer to a warmed serving dish and mix in the reserved radish leaves; they will wilt in the heat. Stir in the shredded preserved lemon rind and taste for seasoning (you might want a little more of the brine). Scatter on the mint leaves and serve.

FROM THE OVEN

I am an inveterate roaster—it's my favorite cooking method—partly because it's easy. You don't have to brown pieces of meat, or nudge the lid on your casserole to regulate the reduction of cooking juices. Beef caramelizes to sweetness, the skin on a chicken becomes crisp with salt and bronzed; you can sense that they will be tender. We mostly associate roasting with meat, but I like it so much as an approach that I've tried it on nearly everything. Its dry heat works on fruit, vegetables, and fish, charring the edges of peach halves and wedges of pumpkin. It intensifies flavor, which is why cottony apricots and insipid tomatoes become something else entirely, their essence—hiding in there the whole time—distilled, and their sweetness brought to the fore.

You have to learn to use your oven well; if you're cooking a main course, it makes sense to shove in a tray of peppers or tomatoes that will see you through the next few days, too. I am nearly always roasting or baking a dish to eat that night and raiding the refrigerator to see what else can be usefully cooked on another shelf at the same time. I even use the oven to cook steaks and pork chops (my steaks and chops are "sear-roasted"; once you've tried this, you'll find it's easier than cooking them on the stovetop and it produces great results).

Originally, roasting wasn't done in a closed box, but in front of a fire, the meat either on the hearth or suspended from a hook, and someone had to move it around to make sure it cooked evenly. It was the price of fuel that led to the development, during the late 18th century in England and in the American colonies, of a "closed hearth," the precursor to the modern oven. Not everyone liked it. Some food writers decried the loss of "proper" roasts claiming, as English writer Dorothy Hartley did, that meat cooked in this closed chamber was now baked rather than roasted. In fact, baking and roasting are both methods of cooking in dry heat, it's what we are cooking that usually dictates the word we use: bread is baked, chickens are roasted. Fat has a role to play in dictating which term is used as well. The difference between a roast potato and a baked one is that the first is cooked in fat.

Roasting—cooking in dry heat—is not the only thing that goes on in the oven. When you cook meat in a covered pot with a little liquid (and vegetables or aromatics), it's called pot-roasting and there are a few recipes in here for pot roasts, too. The redoubtable Anne Willan, in her *Complete Guide to Cookery*, writes that pot-roasting "…is not at all precise. It means to cook in the oven in a covered casserole but with what, and how, is up to the cook." It can be as simple as browning a chicken, then setting it on a bed of chopped onions and herbs, adding a splash of vermouth, and letting the meat make its own juices, or it can be surrounded by more liquid—stock or wine—and larger vegetables (whole waxy potatoes, carrots, and leeks). The vegetables become more than just an accompaniment, as they've cooked in the meat's juices. Apart from the convenience of having meat and vegetables together—so you don't have to cook a side dish—the key thing with this approach is the moistness of the flesh and the exchange of flavors. The moist heat created in the pot produces a very different result from the dry heat of roasting.

There are also many recipes in this book that use an approach somewhere between dry roasting and pot roasting. The protein being roasted—usually chicken thighs or fish—sits on a layer of vegetables moistened with a little stock, alcohol, or water. If you've salted the chicken skin, it will become crisp and you end up with a dish that is part braise, part roast: vegetables imbued with meat juices and a bit of burnished protein on top. There's no carving and the dish can be served straight from the pan. There are also recipes in which rice—long-grain rice or Spanish paella rice—is cooked in the oven in stock, the liquid becoming absorbed by the fattening grains while meat, fish, or vegetables cook on top. To me, these offer the best of all possible worlds, dishes transformed by the heat of the oven that have everything: a golden finish, moist vegetables, and starch.

And don't think that it's always meat that is the star. Chucking vegetables—roots or Mediterranean vegetables, wedges of cabbage, or trays of broccoli—into the oven (once they've been tossed in melted butter or olive oil) is something I do most evenings. If the main dish doesn't include vegetables, I cook them alongside (and these days vegetables are often the main dish, not a supporting act). Even peas, radishes, and string beans can be cooked in the oven. Roasting makes them taste even more like themselves, their character concentrated rather than lost.

When roasting different vegetables together you have to be aware of their different cooking times, adding each vegetable at the right moment (e.g. string beans to roast tomatoes once the tomatoes are becoming caramelized), and you need to cut them to the correct size, too, so they can cook together and be ready at the same time. The more you cook vegetables in the oven, the more you find out what each requires.

Most of the recipes are very straightforward, but there's a couple of things to remember when you're cooking in the oven: bring the food to room temperature beforehand, and heat the oven in advance. An oven thermometer is invaluable. I use it to check the temperature both before cooking—to make sure the oven has hit the temperature to which it's set—and during cooking. Oven temperatures fluctuate. When that happens, I adjust it. I also get my oven calibrated fairly regularly. No matter how stellar your oven, there's a good chance that it's a little hotter or a little cooler than it says it is. You may try recipes in this book and find that it takes a bit longer or, perhaps, less time to get the required result. Make a note of this, so that you know what to do the next time.

Cooking food in the oven is easy, but it brings another pleasure too; although I know I'm the one who has smeared the bird with butter, mixed the crumble with my fingers or halved the peppers and turned them over in olive oil, I always feel, when I take food out of the oven, that someone else has cooked it. I've basically been drinking wine and enjoying the smell as it starts to permeate the kitchen; the cooking has done itself.

When you put meat or a pile of roasted vegetables on a platter, you don't feel that you are serving it, but that it is serving itself: it looks like an offering. This is one of the reasons I don't think cooking is difficult, or it certainly doesn't have to be. The alchemy of heat is a gift. With only a little knowledge—and gradual practice—you can learn how to use the warmth within that closed box.

BAKED PEPPERS STUFFED WITH GOAT CHEESE, RICOTTA & BASIL

This can be a side dish, an appetizer, or even a main course, if it's served with another vegetable dish. The peppers are good with roast lamb and chicken, too. You can add chopped artichoke hearts—the ones you buy in olive oil in jars—to the stuffing as well.

Preheat the oven to 375°F.

Halve the peppers, deseed them, brush them with olive oil, and put them into a gratin dish from which they can be served.

Drain the ricotta and the goat cheese (there can be a little moisture lying on top of them). Mix together all 3 cheeses with seasoning, the basil, egg, and garlic, gently mashing. Add the pine nuts if you are using them.

Spoon the mixture into the pepper halves and bake for 40 minutes. The filling should be golden and souffléd and the peppers completely tender when pierced with a sharp knife. If they're not ready, return them to the oven for an extra 5–10 minutes, then test again.

SERVES 6 AS A SIDE DISH, OR AS AN APPETIZER, OR AS PART OF A SPREAD OF DISHES

6 medium bell peppers

a little extra virgin olive oil

5½oz ricotta (fresh rather than ultra-pasteurized, if possible)

10½oz soft goat cheese

1 cup finely grated Parmesan cheese

sea salt flakes and freshly ground black pepper

1 cup basil leaves, torn

1 large egg

1 garlic clove, crushed

1 tablespoon toasted pine nuts (optional)

MOROCCAN ROASTED VEGETABLES WITH LABNEH

If you don't want to serve the labneh—though it's only drained yogurt that you leave in the refrigerator overnight to make itself— then just stir a couple of chopped preserved lemons into a bowl of Greek yogurt and serve that alongside the vegetables instead.

Start the labneh the day before. Put the yogurt into a piece of cheesecloth or a brand new all-purpose kitchen cloth set in a sieve over a bowl. Stir in some salt and pepper. Pull the fabric up round the yogurt to make a "bag." Put the whole thing—including the bowl to catch the liquid that drains out—in the refrigerator for 24 hours. Give it a gentle squeeze every so often. You'll get a firm yogurt "cheese."

Preheat the oven to 400°F.

Cut the squash into wedges (I don't peel it, as the skin softens enough during roasting to be edible) and remove the seeds. Divide between 2 roasting pans, then do the same with the onions, cauliflower, and potatoes. The vegetables need to be able to lie in a single layer, with room to add the tomatoes later. Season, add the chilies, ginger, cumin, and harissa, and drizzle everything with 5 tablespoons of the olive oil. Turn the vegetables so they get covered in the flavorings and oil. Roast for 20 minutes.

Stir in the chickpeas and garlic, add the tomatoes, and drizzle with the rest of the olive oil. Roast for a final 20 minutes, or until the vegetables are tender and slightly charred in places. Check the seasoning.

Transfer the vegetables to a warmed platter or shallow bowl. Squeeze over the lemon juice and scatter with the cilantro and shredded preserved lemon rind. Serve the vegetables and labneh on their own—the dish already contains a starch in the potatoes—or with couscous.

SERVES 6

FOR THE LABNEH

¾ cup Greek yogurt

sea salt flakes and freshly ground black pepper

FOR THE VEGETABLES

4½lbs winter squash or pumpkin

3 onions, cut into thick wedges

2–2½lbs cauliflower florets

1lb creamer potatoes, scrubbed and quartered

2–3 red Fresno chilies, halved, seeded, and thinly sliced

1¼in fresh ginger, peeled and finely grated

½ tablespoon ground cumin

1 tablespoon harissa

7 tablespoons extra virgin olive oil

2 x 15oz cans of chickpeas, drained and rinsed

4 garlic cloves, finely sliced

½lb cherry tomatoes

juice of ½ lemon

½ cup chopped cilantro leaves, to serve

3 preserved lemons, rind only, shredded, to serve

couscous, to serve (optional)

OREGANO-ROASTED EGGPLANTS
WITH ANCHOVY & CHILI SAUCE

Eggplants roast to a lovely velvety softness and can take any flavors you care to throw at them. Despite their subtlety, they seem to be able to hold their own. This anchovy sauce is simple and is also excellent with roast tomatoes and roast peppers: salty and sweet.

Preheat the oven to 400°F.

Halve the eggplants and cut a cross-hatched pattern in the flesh of each one, without cutting all the way through to the skin (this helps the heat to penetrate better). Put them on to a rimmed baking sheet—line it with parchment paper or foil if you want—and smear the olive oil evenly all over the cut surfaces. Toss in the oregano, too, and salt and pepper. Turn the eggplants over with your hands, making sure the seasoning and some of the herb leaves go into the flesh.

Roast, cut side up, for about 40 minutes, or until the eggplants are completely tender right through and golden. Squeeze the lemon juice over the top.

To make the sauce, pound the rosemary and garlic in a mortar, then add the anchovies and crush to a paste. Gradually add the lemon juice and then the olive oil, a little at a time, grinding as you go. You aren't making a mayonnaise—so don't expect this to emulsify, you'll be left with a lumpy "sauce"—but the pounding melds all the elements together. Add the chili and set aside. The longer the sauce sits with the chili, the hotter it will become.

Serve the eggplants with the sauce, either on the side or spooned over the top. You need good bread with this, to mop up all the juices.

SERVES 4 AS A SIDE DISH

FOR THE EGGPLANTS

4¾lb globe eggplants

4 tablespoons extra virgin olive oil

leaves from 3 oregano sprigs, torn

sea salt flakes and freshly ground black pepper

juice of ½ lemon

good crusty bread, to serve

FOR THE SAUCE

leaves from 2 rosemary sprigs

2 garlic cloves, chopped

14 anchovies, drained of oil

juice of 1 lemon, or to taste

4 tablespoons extra virgin olive oil

1 red Fresno chili, halved, seeded, and chopped, plus more if you want it hotter

BAKED FENNEL WITH CRUSHED RED PEPPER & PARMESAN CHEESE

SERVES 6–8 AS
A SIDE DISH

4 fennel bulbs

3 tablespoons extra virgin
olive oil

2 garlic cloves, finely grated

3 teaspoons fennel seeds,
coarsely crushed in a mortar

3 teaspoons crushed red
pepper

sea salt flakes and freshly
ground black pepper

½ cup finely grated
Parmesan cheese

*I used to blanch fennel before roasting it, but if the oven is
really hot, you don't need to. This is one of my favorite side dishes.
I could eat it by the plateful. To make it into a main course,
serve it with burrata, your favorite extra virgin olive oil,
and warm focaccia. As a side dish, it works well with roast lamb,
chicken, and fish.*

Preheat the oven to 400°F.

Trim the tips of the fennel bulbs, halve the bulbs and remove any thicker
or discolored outer leaves (reserve any little fronds you find). Cut each half
into ¾–1in thick wedges, keeping them intact at the base. Toss in a bowl with
the olive oil, garlic, fennel seeds, crushed red pepper, any reserved fennel fronds,
and plenty of seasoning. Put into a gratin dish and cover tightly with foil.

Bake for about 20 minutes (the undersides should turn pale gold), then
remove the foil, sprinkle on the Parmesan, and return to the oven for a final
10–15 minutes, or until the fennel is tender (check it by piercing a piece with
a sharp knife) and the top is golden.

BUTTER-ROAST EGGPLANT & TOMATOES WITH FREEKEH & KOCH-KOCHA

More buttery eggplant... and what a revelation this dish is. There's nothing to it, it's just eggplants and tomatoes roasted with garlicky butter, but it tastes more complex than you would expect. The cooked freekeh becomes lovely and sticky round the edges as it bakes in the vegetable juices, too. Koch-kocha is an Ethiopian sauce, a bit like Yemeni zhug. You don't need to get grains of paradise or ajwain for it (some bashed caraway seeds will do instead of the ajwain and grains of paradise are peppery and coriander-like, so substitute toasted and some crushed coriander seeds). You can buy both online, though. I've used oil in the sauce, but you can just use water.

Preheat the oven to 400°F.

Pierce each eggplant with the tip of a knife—you don't have to remove the tops—and cut the tomatoes in half. Put them into a roasting pan or a shallow casserole 12in in diameter; they don't have to *quite* lie in a single layer but they should almost do so.

Melt the butter in a saucepan and add the garlic. Cook over a low heat for a few minutes, then pour the butter all over the vegetables, turning them over. Season and sprinkle each tomato half with a little sugar if they aren't very sweet; if you have great tomatoes you won't need it.

Roast for 30 minutes, turning the eggplants over once during this time.

For the koch-kocha sauce, simply put everything into a food processor and whizz until smooth.

Add the freekeh to the roasting pan, pushing it down under the vegetables (you don't want it sprinkled on top of them). Return to the oven for a final 5–10 minutes, or until the tomatoes are caramelized, the eggplants are tender right through, and the freekeh has become slightly sticky at the edges. Serve the dish with the sauce, a big bowl of plain yogurt, and good bread.

SERVES 4

FOR THE VEGETABLES AND FREEKEH

2¼lbs baby eggplants

2¼lbs plum tomatoes

7 tablespoons unsalted butter

12 garlic cloves, thickly sliced

sea salt flakes and freshly ground black pepper

a little light brown sugar (optional, only if your tomatoes aren't sweet)

scant 2 cups cooked freekeh

plain yogurt, to serve

good bread, to serve

FOR THE KOCH-KOCHA

½ green bell pepper, halved, seeded, and roughly chopped

4 cups cilantro leaves

1 red Fresno chili and 1 green chili, halved and deseeded

1¼in fresh ginger, peeled and finely grated

juice of 1 lime

½ tablespoon cider vinegar or white wine vinegar

1 garlic clove, finely grated

1 teaspoon ground cumin

1 teaspoon ground cardamom

¼ teaspoon grains of paradise, crushed

½ teaspoon ajwain, crushed

7 tablespoons extra virgin olive oil

ROASTED EGGPLANT PURÉE WITH SOFT GOAT CHEESE, SMOKED ALMONDS, CHILI & ROSEMARY

SERVES 6 AS A SIDE DISH

3¾lb globe eggplants

5 tablespoons extra virgin olive oil

2 teaspoons harissa

sea salt flakes and freshly ground black pepper

2 garlic cloves (not too large), finely grated

juice of ½ lemon, or to taste

3½oz goat curd or soft creamy goat cheese

1 tablespoon smoked almonds, roughly chopped (you want quite big bits)

2 red Fresno chilies, halved, seeded, and very thinly sliced

leaves from 1 rosemary sprig, chopped

warm flatbread or toasted sourdough bread, to serve

Another dish that shows off the soft, collapsing flesh of roast eggplants. You could finish this purée in other ways: with feta cheese, melted butter, and chopped dill, or with capers tossed in a vinaigrette with chopped anchovies and olives.

Preheat the oven to 400°F.

Put the eggplants in a roasting pan and brush lightly with some of the olive oil. Pierce each a few times with the tines of a fork. Roast for 40–45 minutes, or until the eggplants are completely soft and look a bit deflated.

Leave until cool enough to handle, then slit the skins and scoop the flesh out into a bowl. Chop the flesh (it will be totally soft, you just need to break it down a bit). Mash, and add about 3½ tablespoons of the oil, the harissa, salt, pepper, garlic, and lemon juice to taste. Put this into a warmed serving bowl and scatter the goat cheese on top.

Heat the remaining extra virgin olive oil in a frying pan and quickly fry the smoked almonds, chilies, and rosemary together (you just want to take the rawness off the chilies a little). Pour this over the roast eggplants and serve with bread.

SERVES 4

4 zucchini

1lb small waxy potatoes,
scrubbed and quartered

⅔lb cherry tomatoes

12 scallions, trimmed

3 tablespoons extra virgin
olive oil

sea salt flakes and freshly
ground black pepper

leaves from 3 thyme sprigs,
plus 5 whole thyme sprigs

½ teaspoon crushed red
pepper (optional)

¾ tablespoon smoked
paprika, plus more to serve

4 garlic cloves, finely grated

½lb string beans, stem ends
removed

6–8 extra-large eggs

Greek yogurt, to serve
(optional)

SMOKED PAPRIKA-BAKED ZUCCHINI, TOMATOES & STRING BEANS WITH EGGS

This is a blueprint for baked eggs and vegetables. The flavors here are quite Spanish (you can also add sautéed chorizo to the dish), but you can make a completely different version by leaving out the smoked paprika and adding slices of prosciutto and grated Parmesan or pecorino cheese along with the eggs.

Preheat the oven to 400°F.

Trim the ends from the zucchini and cut them into ¼in thick slices. Put all the vegetables except the string beans into a shallow casserole, ideally about 12in across, or a roasting pan in which they can all lie in a single layer. Add 2 tablespoons of the olive oil, the seasoning, thyme, crushed red pepper (if you want heat), smoked paprika, and garlic. Toss everything together and bake for 30 minutes, turning the vegetables over a couple of times.

Toss the string beans with the remaining oil and scatter them on top of the other vegetables. Return to the oven for 8 minutes.

Break the eggs on top, season, and return the casserole or pan to the oven for a final 8 minutes or so. The eggs should be cooked.

Serve straight from the pan, sprinkling the eggs with a little more paprika, if you like. If you've made it very spicy—and I often do—a bowl of Greek yogurt on the side is good.

SERVES 4 AS AN
APPETIZER, OR AS PART OF
A SPREAD OF DISHES

⅔lb asparagus spears, of medium thickness

extra virgin olive oil

sea salt flakes and freshly ground black pepper

4½oz ricotta cheese (fresh rather than ultra-pasteurized, if possible)

pecorino cheese, or Parmesan cheese, shaved

ROASTED ASPARAGUS WITH RICOTTA & PECORINO CHEESE

The simplest of dishes and without the hassle of trying (and failing) to prop your asparagus spears up against the side of a saucepan. The stalks should ideally be about the same thickness, so that they're all ready at the same time. If you get good fresh ricotta—not ultra-pasteurized stuff—this is food fit for the gods.

Preheat the oven to 425°F.

Trim the woody ends from the asparagus spears, put them on an sheet pan with a slight lip, and drizzle with olive oil. Season with salt.

Roast for 10–12 minutes, or until the asparagus spears are tender (test one of the thickest with the tip of a sharp knife).

Put the asparagus on a serving plate. Scatter the ricotta in nuggets over the top, followed by the shaved pecorino or Parmesan cheese. Season with salt and pepper, pour on more olive oil, and serve immediately.

TOMATO, GOAT CHEESE & OLIVE CLAFOUTIS WITH BASIL

I'd only ever made sweet clafoutis until I thought about baking this dish and then, suddenly, it seemed obvious. It's a bit like a quiche without the pastry, only softer because it doesn't have to hold its shape in quite the same way as a tart filling. You might think this is light—and it is—but it's also deceptively rich and filling. I don't serve anything with it except some good bread.

Preheat the oven to 400°F.

Put the tomatoes into a gratin dish with the olive oil and season them. Turn them over so the surfaces are all coated in a little oil. Roast for 20–30 minutes, or until the tomatoes are soft and slightly shrunken. Take out of the oven and leave to sit on a work surface.

Reduce the oven temperature to 375°F.

Put the eggs, egg yolks, flour, milk, and cream into a food processor, season well, and whizz. Stir in the Parmesan and garlic.

Scatter the olives over the tomatoes and crumble on the goat cheese.

Pour the batter over the tomatoes, olives, and cheese and bake for 30 minutes, until the custard is puffed, golden, and just set in the middle. Leave it for 5 minutes to settle: it will sink a little once it has sat for a while. Scatter over the basil and serve.

1lb mixed cherry and plum tomatoes, halved or quartered, depending on size

1½ tablespoons extra virgin olive oil

sea salt flakes and freshly ground black pepper

4 large eggs, plus 2 large egg yolks

⅓ cup all-purpose flour

scant 1 cup milk

1¼ cups heavy cream

generous ½ cup finely grated Parmesan cheese

1 garlic clove, finely grated

2 tablespoons chopped pitted black olives

7oz soft goat cheese, crumbled

⅓ cup basil leaves, torn

ROAST CORN, ZUCCHINI, & PEPPERS WITH CUMIN, CHILI, SOUR CREAM & AVOCADO

SERVES 4 WITH
SOMETHING STARCHY
ON THE SIDE, OR
6–8 AS A SIDE DISH

FOR THE VEGETABLES

4 ears of corn

5 zucchini, cut into 3in-long batons

2 red bell peppers, halved, seeded, and cut into broad strips

1 green chili and 2 red Fresno chillies, halved, seeded, and very thinly sliced

1 tablespoon ground cumin

¾ teaspoon ground cinnamon

2 teaspoons dried oregano (preferably Mexican oregano, but regular will do)

4 garlic cloves, finely grated

¼ cup extra virgin olive oil

sea salt flakes and freshly ground black pepper

scant ½ cup cilantro leaves

TO SERVE

2 avocados

juice of 1 lime, plus lime wedges to serve

⅔ cup sour cream

3½oz crumbled cheese, such as *queso fresco* or feta

rice, quinoa, or tortillas

I love roast corn. Before I first cooked it this way, I couldn't see the point of it, but now it's the only type of corn I want. Roasting condenses its sweetness, but it also gives it a toasted "popcorn" flavor. If you can get slim young zucchini you only need to halve them lengthwise, you don't have to cut them into batons, but they vary a lot throughout the season and you probably won't have much choice in what you buy. It's important to roast the corn on its own, not with the other vegetables, otherwise the moisture in the zucchini and peppers won't allow the corn to toast properly. Serve with warm corn or flour tortillas, rice, or quinoa.

Preheat the oven to 400°F.

Cut the pointed tip off one ear of corn. Hold it standing up in a roasting pan. Using a sharp knife, cut down the sides, removing the kernels as you work around. (Try to keep some in strips; cut close to the core to achieve this.) Repeat with the other ears.

Put the zucchini and peppers into another roasting pan. In a small bowl, mix together the chilies, spices, oregano, garlic, olive oil, and seasoning. Mix two-thirds of this with the zucchini and peppers (reserve the rest of the mixture), tossing with your hands so that all the vegetables get coated.

Roast the zucchini and peppers in the oven for 20 minutes, then turn them over. Toss the rest of the oil and spices with the corn, season, and roast that, in its separate pan, alongside the other vegetables for a final 20 minutes.

Halve and pit the avocados. Squeeze lime juice all over the surfaces and season. Serve the roasted vegetables in a warmed broad, shallow bowl, scattered with the cilantro leaves, along with the halved avocados—people can help themselves to the flesh—the sour cream, cheese, and lime wedges. Serve rice, quinoa, or tortillas on the side.

SERVES 4 AS A STARTER

6 red bell peppers

a little extra virgin olive oil

sea salt flakes and freshly
ground black pepper

2¼oz 'nduja

about 1lb burrata

ciabatta, to serve

ROAST PEPPERS WITH BURRATA & 'NDUJA

You barely need a recipe for this, it's just distinctive ingredients, melting together, each providing a contrast to its neighbor: chili-hot 'nduja that falls apart in the heat of the oven, cold creamy burrata, and charred peppers. Most people, when you serve them a plate of this and some ciabatta to mop up the juices, will just be quiet and eat.

Preheat the oven to 400°F.

Halve the peppers, seed them, and put them into a gratin dish, roasting pan, or a baking sheet with a lip around it. Brush them with olive oil, season, and roast for 20 minutes.

Break the 'nduja into chunks and divide it among the peppers, putting it inside them. Roast for a final 10 minutes.

When they're cooked, the pepper skins should be slightly blistered and a little charred in places. Leave them until they're cool enough to handle, then tear them or leave them whole—whichever you prefer—and divide them among 4 plates. Drain the burrata, tear it, and serve it alongside the peppers and 'nduja. Serve some ciabatta on the side.

BEETS &
BITTER GREENS

AUTUMN & WINTER
VEGETABLES

ROASTED AUTUMN VEGETABLES WITH WALNUT-MISO SAUCE

The sauce here is rather like a vegetarian version of the Piedmontese anchovy sauce, bagna cauda *(though it's even more umami-packed). It's not one of those vegetable recipes that feels like a side dish, where you keep searching for the focus, but has enough different flavors and textures from each vegetable to be layered and surprising.*

Preheat the oven to 400°F.

Trim the carrots at the top and tips (if there are long straggly bits on the tips). Leave the green tufts if there are any, but wash them really well. If you haven't been able to get slim carrots, then halve them along their length.

Peel the celery root and cut it into wedges about ¾in thick. Put all the vegetables—except the Belgian endive—into a couple of roasting pans, or sheet pans that have a lip all the way around, in which they can lie in a single layer. Add the olive oil, season (don't use too much salt, as the sauce will be salty), and toss everything around with your hands. Roast for 40 minutes, until tender and slightly scorched, turning them once. Quarter the Belgian endive heads and add halfway through, tossing them in the oil.

Make the sauce. Pound the walnuts in a mortar—or pulse-blend in a food processor—until you have a mixture that is part finely ground and part chunky.

Pour the olive oil into a saucepan set over a very gentle heat. Add the miso and whisk it together: the miso will stay in little globules separate from the oil, but that's normal. Add the chili and garlic and simmer very gently for about 5 minutes, stirring every so often. The garlic must not color. Stir in the walnuts and cook for another 2 minutes.

Transfer the vegetables to a warmed platter. Either spoon the sauce over the top, or serve it on the side.

SERVES 4

FOR THE VEGETABLES

10 thin carrots from a bunch with greens attached, in mixed colors if possible

1lb 2oz celery root

1lb 2oz butternut squash or pumpkin, seeded, and cut into wedges about 1¼in thick

3 large white or red onions, cut into wedges

¼ cup extra virgin olive oil

sea salt flakes and freshly ground black pepper

3 Belgian endives, red or white (or a mixture)

FOR THE SAUCE

½ cup walnut pieces

1½ cups extra virgin olive oil (a fruity rather than a grassy one)

5 tablespoons red miso paste

½ teaspoon crushed red pepper

3 fat garlic cloves, finely grated

MELTING BAKED ONIONS WITH PARMESAN CHEESE & CREAM

SERVES 6 AS A SIDE DISH,
OR AS PART OF A SPREAD
OF DISHES

6 onions, about ⅓lb each

5 tablespoons unsalted
butter

sea salt flakes and freshly
ground black pepper

¼ cup extra virgin olive oil

handful of thyme sprigs

8oz or 1 cup crème fraîche

1 cup finely grated Parmesan
cheese

Eating these is like having your own little bowl of cheesy onion soup. Don't try to hurry them, they need to cook slowly. You could use Gruyère instead of Parmesan, or go more Eastern European and drizzle on butter in which you've sautéed caraway seeds or paprika and serve with nuggets of bacon, or Quark or sour cream, and smoked grated cheese. There are loads of possibilities, but the onions are sweet, so they do need something salty. Serve as a side dish for meat (something plain like roast chicken is best), or as a main course with another vegetable dish.

Preheat the oven to 350°F.

Remove the outer skins of the onions, but leave on at least 1 layer of papery skin. Trim the bottoms a little so that they can sit upright in the oven.

Rub some butter over the bottom of each onion and season the exposed flesh. Set them on a double-thick layer of foil or parchment paper (big enough to come up around the onions and be twisted to seal later). Pour a little olive oil on each onion and add a few thyme sprigs. Seal the parcel and transfer to a roasting pan.

Bake for 1¾ hours. The inside of the onions should be completely soft, with juices all round the bottom. Open the package, split each onion open, season, spoon some of the cooking juices inside, and add a spoonful of crème fraîche and some cheese.

ROASTED SPICED EGGPLANTS, PUMPKIN & TOMATOES WITH COCONUT & GREEN CHUTNEY

This dish can be simple or slightly more complicated. The spice paste has warmth from the ginger and heat from the chili and it's hard to believe the effect it has on the vegetables: you really can just eat them with a bowl of yogurt. But make the chutney, too, and you have a feast (the chutney is also great with white and oily fish or with chicken, either on the side or stuffed under the chicken skin before roasting). The chutney can be completely savory or slightly sweet, depending on what you want to serve it with.

Preheat the oven to 400°F.

Put everything for the spice paste into a food processor and whizz. Scrape into a bowl (don't clean the food processor yet).

Halve the tomatoes and put them in a roasting pan in which they can lie in a single layer. Spoon some of the spice paste on top of each, then turn them to make sure they get well coated all over, arranging them so they're all cut side up. Halve the eggplants lengthwise and cut a cross-hatched pattern in the flesh side, without cutting all the way through (this helps the heat to penetrate). Put them in a large roasting pan that has enough room for the pumpkin to fit in later in a single layer and rub them with half the remaining spice paste, ending cut sides up. Roast both trays for 20 minutes.

Seed the pumpkin and cut into slices—there's no need to peel them, as the skin softens while they're in the oven—about 1in thick at their thickest part. Rub over the rest of the spice paste. If the mixture doesn't go quite far enough (though it should), add a little more olive oil. Add the pumpkin slices to the eggplant pan.

Return the pumpkin and eggplant pan to the oven and roast for 20 minutes, turning the pumpkin slices over halfway through this time. The vegetables

continued >

SERVES 4

FOR THE SPICE PASTE

1½in fresh ginger, peeled and chopped

10 garlic cloves, chopped

3 red Fresno chilies, halved, seeded, and chopped

1 shallot, roughly chopped

seeds from 10 cardamom pods

sea salt flakes and freshly ground black pepper

4 teaspoons light brown sugar

juice of 2 limes

6 tablespoons extra virgin olive oil, plus more if needed

FOR THE VEGETABLES

8 plum tomatoes

4 globe eggplants, a generous 1lb each

2lb pumpkin or winter squash

cilantro leaves, to serve (optional)

2½ tablespoons unsweetened coconut flakes, toasted

plain yogurt, and warmed naan bread, to serve

should now be ready—tender and golden—but keep an eye on the tomatoes so they don't overcook (they may only take 30 minutes cooking time in total, so check on them when you turn the pumpkin slices). They should still hold their shape, not completely collapse.

To make the chutney, put everything for it in the food processor (you don't need to wash the bowl after the spice paste) and pour in ⅓ cup water. Whizz. If you want the chutney to be a little sweet, add the sugar. Taste for seasoning and sharpness, then scrape into a bowl.

Put all the vegetables on a warmed platter and scatter over the cilantro leaves with the toasted coconut flakes.

Serve with the chutney and a bowl of yogurt (regular yogurt, for its sourness, rather than the Greek variety), and warmed naan bread.

FOR THE CHUTNEY

1 teaspoon ground cumin

1¾oz cilantro, any thicker stalks removed

Generous 1 cup mint leaves

Packed 1 cup baby spinach

3½oz creamed coconut, from a block, crumbled or coarsely grated

1 green chili, halved, deseeded and chopped

3 garlic cloves, chopped

1in fresh ginger, peeled and chopped

finely grated zest of 1 lime and juice of 3 limes, or to taste

sea salt, to taste

1 teaspoon superfine sugar, if you want a sweet version

AN OVEN FULL OF POTATOES...

As with the novel, the demise of the potato is much discussed but never actually materializes, at least not in my house. This is not an exhaustive list, but it should help you cook potatoes that will go with Mediterranean dishes, Eastern European food, Indian, Greek, or sort-of-French recipes. You can stick them in the oven on the shelf below (or alongside) whatever starchless main course you're cooking. The first recipe is the most basic and can take endless simple variations. You do have to make sure your potatoes are cut to the correct (and roughly the same) size, though these are forgiving rather than exacting dishes. Cooked potatoes are tender and the tip of a knife will tell you whether they're ready or not.

ROSEMARY, GARLIC & OLIVE OIL-ROAST POTATOES

The most basic throw-it-in-the-oven potatoes. I make this all the time, though sometimes leave out the garlic. Take 1½lbs of potatoes—waxy or russet, though they will give you different results (I usually go for waxy)—and cut them into chunks just a little smaller than a walnut. Separate the cloves from 2 heads of garlic, but don't peel them. Strip the leaves from 2 rosemary sprigs (have another 3 whole sprigs). Put all of this in a roasting pan in which everything can lie in a single layer and add 2–3 tablespoons of extra virgin olive oil, 1 tablespoon of balsamic vinegar, salt, and pepper. Roast in an oven preheated to 400°F for 35 minutes, tossing them a couple of times as they cook. Smoked paprika or crushed red pepper (or both) are a good addition. SERVES 4

THYME ROAST POTATOES WITH ONIONS, BLACK OLIVES & GOAT CHEESE

Halve or quarter 1½lbs of waxy creamer potatoes. Toss them in a roasting pan in which they can lie in a single layer, with 2 red onions, cut into wedges, 3 tablespoons of extra virgin olive oil, 1 tablespoon of balsamic vinegar, salt, pepper, and 8 thyme sprigs. Roast in an oven preheated to 400°F for 35 minutes, shaking halfway through. About 7 minutes before the end of cooking time, add 3 tablespoons of small black olives (unpitted are fine) and 5½oz of goat cheese, broken into chunks. SERVES 4

ROAST POTATOES WITH FETA CHEESE, GREEN CHILIES, & MINT

Halve or quarter 1½lbs of waxy creamer potatoes. Put them in a roasting pan in which they can lie in a single layer, toss in 3 tablespoons of extra virgin olive oil, and season. Put them in an oven preheated to 400°F and cook for 20 minutes. Take them out and add 1–2 green chilies —depending on how hot you want the dish to be—halved, seeded, and finely shredded. Toss everything around in the oil and return to the oven for a final 15–20 minutes. Add ⅓ cup of crumbled feta cheese and the torn leaves from 6 mint sprigs. Squeeze lemon or lime juice over the top and serve. SERVES 4

ROAST POTATOES WITH BACON, SCALLIONS, PAPRIKA & CARAWAY

Halve or quarter 1½lbs of waxy creamer potatoes. Put them in a roasting pan in which they can lie in a single layer and add 1 large onion, cut into wedges about ½in thick, ½lb of ¼in-thick bacon lardons, 2 teaspoons of caraway seeds, 2 teaspoons of sweet paprika, and 2 tablespoons of extra virgin olive oil. Toss everything around and roast for 20 minutes in an oven preheated to 400°F, then brush a little oil on 16 thin trimmed scallions. Toss the vegetables and bacon, lay the scallions on top, and roast for 15 minutes. The potatoes should be tender and the scallions soft and a little charred. SERVES 4–6

ROAST POTATOES & TOMATOES WITH ANCHOVIES, CAPERS, FENNEL & ROSEMARY

Halve or quarter 1½lbs of waxy creamer potatoes. Put them in a roasting pan in which they can lie in a single layer and toss them with 2 tablespoons of extra virgin olive oil, the roughly chopped leaves of 2 rosemary sprigs, ¼–½ teaspoon of crushed red pepper, and ¼ teaspoon of fennel seeds (bash the fennel a little in a mortar first). Roast in an oven preheated to 400°F for 15 minutes, then add ⅓lb of cherry tomatoes. Toss them and roast for another 15 minutes. Add 10 chopped anchovies, plus 1 tablespoon of oil from the anchovy can or jar, and 2 tablespoons of rinsed and drained capers, patted dry. Toss everything again and roast in the oven for a final 5 minutes. Taste. The capers and anchovies are salty, so you shouldn't need seasoning. SERVES 4

BABY POTATOES & LEEKS BAKED IN PAPER WITH HERB BUTTER

Mash 2 tablespoons of unsalted butter with 1 tablespoon each of finely chopped chives and flat leaf parsley leaves (chervil is good, too, if you can get it) and a splash of dry white vermouth. Halve or quarter 1lb 2oz of waxy creamer potatoes. Trim 2 leeks, discard the coarse outer leaves, and cut into lengths of about 1¼in. Cut out 6 rectangles of parchment paper, each about 14 x 12in. Put the potatoes, leeks, and seasoning in the middle of each piece of paper and add a generous pat of the butter. Bring the edges of the paper together and roll them tightly, allowing some room around the potatoes, then twist the ends so you have sealed parcels. Put on a baking sheet and bake for 35–40 minutes in an oven preheated to 400°F. The packages will puff up and the vegetables should be tender. Serve them in the parcels, so people can open them at the table. SERVES 6

INDIAN-SPICED ROAST POTATOES & CAULIFLOWER

A kind of roasted *aloo gobi*. Cut 1lb 2oz of russet potatoes into chunks the size of a walnut (peel them if you have time) and break a 2lb cauliflower into florets (keep the leaves). Toss the potatoes and cauliflower florets (reserve the leaves) in a bowl with 4 chopped plum tomatoes, 3 teaspoons of cumin seeds, and 1 teaspoon of coriander seeds (toasted in a dry pan for a minute, then crushed a bit). Add 1 teaspoon of mild red Kashmiri chili powder, 1 teaspoon of ground turmeric, and 1¼oz of fresh ginger, peeled and finely grated. Add ¼ cup of peanut oil, salt, and pepper and toss with your hands. Spread out in a large roasting pan or sheet pan (use 2 if you need to) in which everything can lie in a single layer. Roast in an oven preheated to 400°F for 20 minutes, turning every so often. Add 2 garlic cloves, finely grated, and the cauliflower leaves, toss, and roast for a final 10 minutes. The vegetables should be tender and golden. Sprinkle with chopped cilantro leaves and lime juice. SERVES 4–6

ROAST SWEET POTATOES WITH CAYENNE & SPINACH

Wash 3 medium-small sweet potatoes, remove any tufts from the surface, and cut into 1in chunks. Toss in a bowl with 2 tablespoons of extra virgin olive oil, 1 teaspoon of cayenne pepper, salt, and pepper. Transfer to a large sheet pan and put into the top of an oven preheated to 400°F. Roast for 50 minutes, turning once during cooking. Stir in a couple of handfuls of torn spinach leaves— they wilt in the heat of the potatoes—squeeze on the juice of ½ lemon, and serve. You can also add crumbled feta cheese, dill or mint leaves, or chopped olives (green or black) with the spinach. SERVES 4–6

BAKED POTATOES WITH SMOKED TROUT, DILLED BEETS, CRÈME FRAÎCHE & SALMON ROE

It's crazy, I know, but this dish—and it's just a fancy baked potato, really—is one of my favorites in the book. You don't have to have the salmon roe, and it isn't cheap, but I love the little pearls of saltiness that pop in your mouth against the cream and the soft potato flesh.

Preheat the oven to 400°F.

Scrub the potatoes and prick each with a fork. While they are still damp, sprinkle lightly all over with sea salt flakes. This will give a crisp skin (cooking them wrapped in foil will give a soft skin).

Put the potatoes on a baking sheet—not touching—and scatter the sheet with a little water by shaking wet hands over it. Bake for 1–1½ hours; the exact cooking time depends on the size of the potatoes and how many you are cooking at a time (more potatoes will take more time).

To test whether the potatoes are done, press them: they should feel soft under the skin and "give" a little. Pierce with a fine skewer through the center if you want to be sure.

While the potatoes are cooking, roughly chop the beets and toss with the shallot, dill, and a little seasoning.

When the potatoes are ready, split them open, season, and put some butter on both halves.

Fill with the beet mixture and the trout, squeeze lemon juice on top, then add a dollop of crème fraîche and spoon on some salmon roe. Grind some pepper over the top and serve with a few bitter greens.

SERVES 2

2 russet potatoes

sea salt flakes and freshly ground black pepper

2¼oz cooked beets (not pickled)

1 shallot, very finely chopped

½ tablespoon chopped dill, any thicker stalks removed

1 tablespoon unsalted butter

2¾oz smoked trout, flaked

good squeeze of lemon juice

3 tablespoons crème fraîche

scant 1oz salmon roe

bitter greens, such as Treviso or red Belgian endive, to serve

ROASTED CAULIFLOWER WITH PISTACHIO & PRESERVED LEMON RELISH & TAHINI

It took me a while to work out the best way to roast a whole cauliflower. Partly steaming it—which is what happens under the foil here—and then roasting it in butter (which seeps right down into the florets) produces the most tender and deeply flavored result. I've been replacing olive oil with butter quite a lot—it cooks more gently, more richly, the surface of whatever it touches bathing in fat rather than frying in it. The cauliflower becomes tender right through to the middle and turns into a gorgeous golden mass.

Preheat the oven to 425°F.

Carefully trim the cauliflower stalk, as it can be dry, but don't cut away the bottom or the leaves. Put it in a roasting pan in which it fits fairly snugly. Add boiling water to come ½in up the sides and cover tightly with foil. Bake for 30 minutes (check to make sure the water hasn't dried up in this time). The cauliflower should just meet a little resistance when you push a skewer into the center. Pour away any remaining water. Drizzle with the melted butter and 3 tablespoons of the olive oil and season. Roast, uncovered, for 15 minutes, or until the cauliflower is golden and the center is completely tender (test with a skewer).

Beat the tahini in a bowl, adding ⅔ cup water, the lemon juice, the remaining 4 tablespoons of oil, salt and pepper, and the garlic. The mixture will "seize" when you add the lemon juice, but keep beating and you'll break it down into a smooth cream. Check for seasoning and acidity.

For the relish, put the garlic and salt in a mortar and pound until the garlic is completely crushed. Add the pistachios and cilantro and bash everything together, gradually adding the oil and cider vinegar until you have a chunky paste (not a purée). Stir in the honey, preserved lemon rind, and chilies.

Serve the cauliflower on a warmed platter and drizzle the tahini around it. Spoon the cooking juices and some relish on top, serving the rest on the side.

SERVES 4, OR 8 AS A SIDE DISH

FOR THE CAULIFLOWER

1 2½lb cauliflower

3 tablespoons unsalted butter, melted

7 tablespoons extra virgin olive oil

sea salt flakes and freshly ground black pepper

¼ cup tahini

juice of 1 lemon

1 garlic clove, finely grated

FOR THE RELISH

2 garlic cloves, chopped

pinch of sea salt flakes

3½ tablespoons shelled unsalted pistachios

2½ cups chopped cilantro leaves

8 tablespoons extra virgin olive oil

1 tablespoon cider vinegar

1 teaspoon clear honey

2 preserved lemons, rind only, finely shredded

2 green chilies, halved, seeded, and finely shredded

SERVES 6 AS AN APPETIZER
OR AS A SIDE DISH

1 large round cabbage, such
as Savoy

5 tablespoons extra virgin
olive oil, or 3 tablespoons
unrendered pork fat (ask
your butcher, don't use lard)

2½oz sourdough rye bread

3½ tablespoons XO sauce

ROASTED CABBAGE WEDGES
WITH XO CRUMBS

Yes, XO sauce—a sauce made from dried scallops, shrimp, and chili that's popular in Hong Kong—is a specialized ingredient you'll probably have to buy online, but this dish is unique and I'd love you to taste it, without having to make the trip to St Leonard's restaurant in East London where they serve it. The chef there, Andrew Clarke, cooks cabbage wedges with pork fat on an open fire and makes his own XO sauce, but he helped me to work out this simpler version. The rye crumbs, tossed with the XO, are deeply umami (you must use rye crumbs). Who knew cabbage could be this good? I could eat it by the (large) plateful. If XO sauce is an adventure too far (or too expensive) you can still make roast cabbage wedges with a buttermilk dressing (see page 178), scattered with dill or smoked bacon lardons, or rye crumbs and caraway, or grated hard cheese (goat Gouda is gorgeous). You can also serve the wedges very simply, with grated Parmesan cheese.

Preheat the oven to 400°F. Remove any discolored leaves from the cabbage, then halve it and cut into wedges about 1–1¼in thick. Melt the pork fat, if using, in a small saucepan. Put the cabbage into a roasting pan. Add half the olive oil or fat and turn the wedges over in it. Roast for 30 minutes, turning halfway through.

Whizz the rye bread into coarse crumbs. Heat the remaining oil or fat in a large frying pan and, when hot, add the crumbs and sauté them until they're toasted (it's hard to tell by color with rye crumbs, so try to go by texture and smell). Scrape these out onto a large double layer of paper towels to soak up the excess fat. Leave to cool, then transfer to a bowl and toss with the XO sauce, forking it through. (XO sauce isn't just liquid, it also has bits of dried shellfish in it, but you can still mix it in well.)

When the cabbage is tender and slightly caramelized—even a little charred in patches—on each side, serve it with the XO crumbs scattered on top.

ROASTED CAULIFLOWER WITH PROSCIUTTO & TALEGGIO CHEESE

SERVES 2–4, DEPENDING ON APPETITE

1 2½lb cauliflower

a little extra virgin olive oil

sea salt flakes and freshly ground black pepper

4½oz Taleggio cheese, sliced

4 prosciutto slices

generous ¼ cup crème fraîche

2¾oz Gruyère cheese, finely grated

salad greens, to serve

Yes, a cauliflower "steak" (though I refuse to call it that). I wasn't at all sure about roasting slices of cauliflower. It was another of those dishes that seemed to have been created just so we could think of vegetables as if they were meat, rather than being delicious in their own right... but then I made this for my children—the harshest critics—and they loved it. It's a bit of a cross between cheesy cauliflower and veal Cordon Bleu and what's not to like about that? It will never be a steak because it isn't, but I like this just as much.

Preheat the oven to 450°F.

Remove the leaves from the cauliflower. Now remove some of the central core, too—working at the bottom—so that you've removed the dense core (without cutting away so much that the head collapses). Cut the cauliflower in half from top to bottom, then cut off 4 slices—2 from each half—each about ¾in thick. Put these on a baking sheet, brush all over with olive oil, and season. Cover the baking sheet with foil and cook for 12 minutes.

Remove the foil and reduce the oven temperature to 400°F. Roast the cauliflower for another 8 minutes.

Remove from the oven—the pieces should be golden—and turn the slices of cauliflower over. On top of each, lay one-quarter of the Taleggio, then a prosciutto slice, then 1 tablespoon crème fraîche. Sprinkle the slices evenly with the Gruyère and return to the oven.

Roast for another 8 minutes, or until the cauliflower is golden and all the cheese has melted. The cauliflower slices should be completely tender when pierced with a sharp knife.

Serve immediately with lightly dressed salad greens.

OLIVE OIL-ROASTED SWEET & SOUR GREENS WITH RAISINS & PINE NUTS

SERVES 6–8 AS A
SIDE DISH

1 head of radicchio

16 thin scallions, trimmed

sea salt flakes and freshly ground black pepper

½ teaspoon crushed red pepper

4 tablespoons extra virgin olive oil

1½ tablespoons white balsamic vinegar

1lb lacinato/dinosaur kale

2 garlic cloves, very thinly sliced

2 tablespoons raisins, soaked in boiling water for 15 minutes, then drained

2 tablespoons toasted pine nuts

The cooking times for the kale here are crucial; the first time you make it you need to keep an eye on the leaves, because your oven could be slightly hotter or slightly cooler than it says on the dial. They can go from slightly scorched to burned very quickly. If you want a plainer version—not sweet-sour—then just leave out the raisins. In that case, you could finish the greens with shaved Parmesan or pecorino cheese.

Preheat the oven to 425°F.

Halve the radicchio and cut it into wedges. Remove the coarse core from each piece, but don't take away so much that the wedges fall apart. If any of the scallions are thick, halve them lengthwise.

Put the radicchio and the scallions into a roasting pan and add salt and pepper, half the crushed red pepper, half the olive oil, and 1 tablespoon of the white balsamic vinegar. Turn everything over with your hands (don't worry if some of the radicchio leaves break off).

Remove the stems from the lacinato kale and put it into another roasting pan. Add another 1 tablespoon of olive oil and the rest of the white balsamic vinegar and crushed red pepper and season. Put the radicchio in the oven and roast it for 5 minutes, then turn the pieces over and return it to the oven with the pan of kale alongside. Roast for 3 minutes, but no longer: timing is crucial. The kale should be slightly crisp around the edges, but mostly soft.

During this last 3 minutes, heat the remaining 1 tablespoon of olive oil in a frying pan and sauté the garlic until it's golden, then add the drained raisins and warm them through. Toss all the vegetables in a warmed serving dish, scatter with the garlic, raisins, and pine nuts, and serve immediately.

BAKED SWEET POTATOES WITH
AVOCADO & CHIMICHURRI

Sweet, hot, and salty, all the things I love eating together. If you can get hold of queso fresco—*Mexican fresh cheese—use that, but feta is a good (if not perfect) substitute. Chimichurri, traditionally served with steak in Argentina and Uruguay, is most commonly made with parsley, but I like it better with half parsley and half cilantro.*

Preheat the oven to 375°F. Put the sweet potatoes on a metal sheet pan (line it with foil or parchment paper to save on the washing up, as the sugar in sweet potatoes can leach out and caramelize). Bake for 40 minutes, or until soft right through to the center.

Put everything for the chimichurri into a blender and blitz to make a smooth sauce. Taste for seasoning.

Split the sweet potatoes down the center, spoon in the yogurt or sour cream, and sprinkle with the cheese and scallions.

Halve the avocados, remove the pits and the skins, then slice or chop the flesh or scoop it straight onto the potatoes. Squeeze lemon or lime juice on the avocado flesh and season. Spoon on the chimichurri and serve with lime wedges.

SERVES 4

FOR THE VEGETABLES

4 sweet potatoes, about 1¼lbs each, well scrubbed

about ½ cup Greek yogurt or sour cream

¼ cup crumbled sharp-tasting cheese (*queso fresco* or feta)

4 scallions, trimmed and sliced on the diagonal

2 smallish ripe avocados

juice of ½ lemon or 1 lime, plus lime wedges to serve

FOR THE CHIMICHURRI

1 small bunch flat-leaf parsley

scant 1 cup cilantro leaves

leaves from 2 oregano sprigs (omit these if you don't have any)

2 garlic cloves, chopped

juice of ½ lemon

1 teaspoon crushed red pepper

7 tablespoons extra virgin olive oil

sea salt flakes and freshly ground black pepper

ROASTED SUNCHOKES & SCALLIONS WITH CRÈME FRAÎCHE, SHAVED GOUDA & HAZELNUTS

You need fat sunchokes for this, as thinner specimens just aren't fleshy enough. If you can't get high-quality Gouda, or don't want to use it, other hard cheeses (such as an aged Cheddar) work, too. This is a gorgeous combination of flavors; don't leave out the hazelnuts as they really are key. This is one of my favorite dishes in the book.

Preheat the oven to 400°F.

Halve the fatter sunchokes lengthwise and put all of them into a roasting pan in which they can lie in a single layer. Season and toss with half the olive oil. Turn everything over with your hands and roast for about 30 minutes.

Toss the scallions in the rest of the oil and season them. Add them to the roasting pan and cook for a final 8 minutes. The scallions should be tender and the sunchokes completely soft and slightly sticky in places (the sugar in them oozes out in little patches).

Mix together the crème fraîche and the buttermilk or milk. Mixing will make the crème fraîche much thinner. Set aside.

To make a dressing, just mix the wine vinegar, mustard, seasoning, sugar, and both the oils together and beat with a fork. Taste, as you might want to adjust the sweetness or acidity.

Toss the treviso or Belgian endive with the dressing. Put the roast vegetables on a serving platter or shallow dish, scatter the treviso or endive over them, then spoon on the crème fraîche mixture (or serve it on the side). Toss the hazelnuts and shaved cheese on top and serve.

SERVES 4 AS A SIDE DISH
OR AS AN APPETIZER

FOR THE VEGETABLES

1½lbs fat sunchokes, all about the same size

sea salt flakes and freshly ground black pepper

3–4 tablespoons extra virgin olive oil

24 thin scallions

½ cup crème fraîche

2 tablespoons buttermilk or regular whole milk

1 head of treviso or red Belgian endive, leaves separated

3 tablespoons toasted hazelnuts, halved

¼ cup shaved really good-quality Gouda cheese

FOR THE DRESSING

3 teaspoons red wine vinegar, or to taste

smidgen of Dijon mustard, or to taste

pinch of superfine sugar, or to taste

1½ tablespoons extra virgin olive oil (a buttery oil, not a grassy one)

1½ tablespoons hazelnut or walnut oil

ROASTED INDIAN-SPICED VEGETABLES WITH LIME-CILANTRO BUTTER

The next time you crave Indian takeout (usually, for me, on a Friday evening, when I'm exhausted), make this instead. You just need to slice some vegetables, then it's 25 minutes in the oven. It is the simplest, loveliest dish: beautiful (the color of the vegetables, especially with the red-and-green-flecked butter melting over them), earthy, and aromatic. Serve it with plain yogurt (Greek yogurt is too creamy, you want something acidic to cut the sweet vegetables), with nigella seeds sprinkled on top, and some chutney (fresh, see page 106, or bought). You don't really need more starch, but warm naan bread is good, too.

Preheat the oven to 425°F. Get out a huge roasting pan or a half sheet pan with a lip round the edge (the pan I use measures 18 x 13in), or use a couple of smaller pans. Put the pan or pans in the oven to heat up.

Put all the vegetables in a very large bowl and add the garlic, oil, and seasoning. Toast the cumin and coriander seeds in a dry frying pan for about a minute, or until you can smell the spices. Put the spices into a mortar with the turmeric and pound all this together. Add the spices to the vegetables in the bowl and turn everything over in the oil. Take the hot pan or pans out of the oven and tumble the vegetables into them. Roast for 25 minutes, tossing the vegetables around halfway through.

Mash the butter together with the chili, cilantro, lime zest, and lime juice.

When the vegetables are ready, either transfer them to a warmed broad, shallow bowl, or serve them in the pan in which they were cooked. Put pats of the butter all over the top and allow it to melt.

Take the vegetables to the table and serve with plain yogurt and chutney.

SERVES 4

FOR THE VEGETABLES

⅔lb small waxy potatoes, scrubbed and quartered

3 medium-small cooked beets, halved

6 long thin carrots, halved (or 3 large carrots, quartered, if you can't find thin)

1 2¼lb cauliflower, broken into florets, with the leaves

3 parsnips, halved lengthwise

3 garlic cloves, finely grated

5 tablespoons peanut oil

sea salt flakes and freshly ground black pepper

2 teaspoons cumin seeds

2 teaspoons coriander seeds

¾ teaspoon ground turmeric

plain yogurt and chutney, to serve

FOR THE BUTTER

5 tablespoons unsalted butter, at room temperature

1 red Fresno chili, halved, seeded, and finely chopped, or ½ teaspoon crushed red pepper

2 tablespoons finely chopped cilantro leaves

finely grated zest of 1 lime, plus a squeeze of lime juice

ROASTED BRUSSELS SPROUTS WITH APPLE & BACON

I'm cheating here, because this isn't entirely cooked in the oven, but the brief roasting is what helps Brussels sprouts achieve their optimum potential, instead of waterlogging them in a saucepan. I ate a similar dish at Rotisserie Georgette in New York—a restaurant that specializes in roast chicken—then came straight home and made this. It's been a regular in my house ever since, and not just at Christmas.

Preheat the oven to 375°F.

Lay the sprouts in a single layer in 1 or 2 roasting pans. Add 2 tablespoons of olive oil, season, and toss.

Roast for 20 minutes, or until the edges begin to look brown and frazzled (they can turn from frazzled to burned very quickly, so keep an eye on them). They won't cook right through, but will finish cooking later.

Heat the remaining 1 teaspoon oil in a sauté pan and fry the bacon lardons until golden and cooked through. Lift out with a slotted spoon.

Remove all but 1 tablespoon of fat from the pan (fat will have rendered from the bacon). Core the apple and cut it into fine crescents, then add to the pan with the onion. Cook over medium heat until golden and soft (though the apple shouldn't be collapsing). It will take about 5 minutes.

Add the sugar, both vinegars, the wine, and the mustard. Return the bacon and season to taste. Toss well and cook until the wine has reduced by about half, then add the sprouts and cook until they are only just tender, but not floppy (all the juices around them should have reduced).

Toss in the butter, if you're using it. Check the seasoning and serve.

SERVES 6 AS A SIDE DISH

1½lbs Brussels sprouts (any discolored outer leaves removed), trimmed and halved

2¼ tablespoons extra virgin olive oil

sea salt flakes and freshly ground black pepper

½lb bacon lardons

1 large tart apple, such as Granny Smith

1 large onion, cut into fine crescent moons

½ tablespoon light brown sugar

1 tablespoon white balsamic vinegar

1 tablespoon cider vinegar

½ cup dry white wine

3 teaspoons Dijon mustard

1 tablespoon unsalted butter (optional, you may feel this is gilding the lily)

ROASTED MUSHROOMS, SUNCHOKES, & CELERY ROOT WITH BROWN BUTTER & HORSERADISH

SERVES 4 AS PART OF A
SPREAD OF DISHES

1⅓lbs sunchokes, all about
the same size

1lb 2oz celery root, peeled
and cut into ½in wedges

3 tablespoons extra virgin
olive oil

7 tablespoons unsalted
butter, melted, plus 2
tablespoons to serve

sea salt flakes and freshly
ground black pepper

8 Portobello mushrooms,
trimmed

½oz fresh horseradish,
peeled and finely grated,
or to taste

crème fraîche, to serve

*Roast mushrooms, celery root and sunchokes look great together
—a tumble of autumnal beige and brown—and there's a lovely
interplay of sweetness, savory meatiness, and herby flavors.
I always find sunchokes too sweet, and celery root too herbal,
when I have them on their own. This is a great recipe for very cold
weather, when it doesn't seem overly rich, despite the butter and
crème fraîche.*

Preheat the oven to 400°F.

Scrub the sunchokes. You don't need to peel them, but halve any larger ones lengthwise. Put them and the celery root into a roasting pan in which they can lie in a single layer. Mix the oil and the 7 tablespoons melted butter and pour about half over the vegetables. Season and toss, then roast for about 45 minutes in total, turning the vegetables over so they become golden on both sides.

Put the mushrooms into a roasting pan where they can lie in a single layer and pour on the rest of the fat. Turn these over with your hands, too, and roast alongside the celery root and sunchokes until they are dark and shrunken, about 30 minutes. The celery root and sunchokes should be tender when pierced with a sharp knife.

Transfer the vegetables to a warmed platter or bowl; you can either leave the mushrooms whole or tear them roughly.

To serve, heat the 2 tablespoons butter until it is golden brown and smells nutty. Pour this over the vegetables and scatter with the horseradish, adding more if you like its clean heat. Serve with a bowl of crème fraîche.

POMEGRANATE MOLASSES-ROASTED BEETS WITH ORANGES, WALNUTS, DILL & LABNEH

If you don't want to make the labneh here—you need to prepare it the day before—then just serve thick yogurt instead. Blood oranges are especially good, so use them if they're in season. I've suggested buying beets with the leaves attached, but that isn't always possible, so just cook what you can find.

Line a sieve with a piece of cheesecloth or a brand new all-purpose kitchen cloth and set it over a bowl. Add the yogurt and stir in some salt and pepper. Pull the fabric up around the yogurt to make a "bag." Put the whole thing —including the bowl to catch the liquid that drains out—in the refrigerator for 24 hours. Give it a gentle squeeze every so often. You'll get a firm yogurt "cheese."

Preheat the oven to 400°F. Wash and peel the beets, keeping the leaves intact, and halve any that are a bit larger. Put a double layer of foil (big enough to make a tent around the beets) into a roasting pan. Mix the balsamic vinegar, olive oil, pomegranate molasses, and garlic together and season well. Put the beets into the foil and pour this on. Toss, then seal the foil to make a package. Cook in the oven until tender right to the middle. This can take as much as 90 minutes, but start checking after 40 (cooking time for beets varies hugely, but you can make these in advance, as they're served at room temperature).

Whisk together all the ingredients for the dressing, then taste for seasoning. Cut the beets into wedges, keeping any leaves intact, and toss them in a bowl with half the dressing, then transfer to a serving platter. Add the orange segments or slices.

Spoon the rest of the dressing over—only use as much as you need, don't smother the beets—then scatter with the pomegranate seeds, walnuts ,and dill. Break the labneh into chunks and dot it around. (If you're using thick yogurt instead, dot spoonfuls here and there, or serve it on the side.)

SERVES 8 AS A SIDE DISH

FOR THE LABNEH AND VEGETABLES

⅔ cup Greek yogurt

sea salt flakes and freshly ground black pepper

3⅓lbs medium-small beets with leaves

2 tablespoons white balsamic vinegar

3 tablespoons extra virgin olive oil

2 tablespoons pomegranate molasses

1 garlic clove, finely grated

3 small oranges, skin, pith and seeds removed, cut into neat segments or slices

seeds from ½ pomegranate

2 tablespoons roughly chopped toasted walnuts

leaves from a small bunch of dill, roughly chopped

FOR THE DRESSING

1 tablespoon white balsamic vinegar

1 teaspoon harissa (or more, depending how hot you want it)

5 tablespoons extra virgin olive oil

½ teaspoon clear honey

½ tablespoon pomegranate molasses

ROASTED SQUASH & TOFU WITH SOY, HONEY, CHILI & GINGER

SERVES 6 WITH RICE, OR AS A SIDE DISH

1lb extra-firm tofu

2lb winter squash

3 tablespoons clear honey

⅓ cup soy sauce

2 teaspoons crushed red pepper

¾in fresh ginger, peeled and finely grated

8 tablespoons peanut oil, divided

sea salt flakes and freshly ground black pepper

6 garlic cloves, very thinly sliced

3 teaspoons toasted sesame seeds

2 scallions, trimmed and sliced on the diagonal

juice of ½ lime

I love the flavors here: sweet and hot. This can be served as a side dish, or as a main course with rice on the side. It doesn't strictly need a sauce, but a hot Asian dressing (see page 194) would be excellent, if you want that.

Preheat the oven to 400°F.

Drain the tofu and cut it into ½in-thick slices. Put a double layer of paper towels on a chopping board, add the tofu, then put another double layer of paper towels on top. Place another chopping board on top of this and weight it. Leave for 20 minutes to press out excess moisture.

Halve and seed the squash and cut it into wedges about ½–¾in thick. In a small bowl, mix the honey, soy sauce, crushed red pepper, ginger, and 5 tablespoons of the oil together.

Divide the squash between 2 roasting pans—you can line them with parchment paper if you want, because it makes the dishes easier to clean—and spoon two-thirds of the soy sauce mixture over it. Turn the squash slices over with your hands.

Cut the tofu slices in half and put them in a smaller roasting pan. Spoon the rest of the soy-sauce mixture over this, turning the pieces in it. Season the squash and tofu and roast in the oven for 15 minutes.

Turn the squash and tofu chunks over. Mix the remaining oil with the garlic and spoon over the squash, then roast with the tofu for a final 10–15 minutes, until the tofu is dark and the squash is burnished and completely tender.

Arrange the squash and tofu on a warmed serving plate, scatter with the sesame seeds and scallions, and squeeze over the lime juice. Serve.

ROASTED CELERY ROOT & SPROUTS WITH BACON, CHESTNUTS & PRUNES

It doesn't have to be eaten just during the festive season, but this dish does shout "CHRISTMAS" rather loudly. You need really good-quality moist prunes, so, as you're not shelling out for fillet of beef or the like here, buy Agen prunes if you can.

Preheat the oven to 400°F.

Peel the celery root and cut it into chunks no bigger than the size of the halved sprouts (larger chunks won't cook through in time). Toss it in a large roasting tin with salt and pepper, half the oil, and all the vinegar and thyme.

Roast for 20 minutes, then stir the celery root around and add the sprouts, onion, pancetta, and the rest of the oil.

Roast for another 10 minutes, then add the chestnuts, prunes, sherry, maple syrup, and butter, and toss the vegetables around.

Cook for a final 10 minutes, then serve.

SERVES 4 AS A SIDE DISH

1⅓lbs celery root

sea salt flakes and freshly ground black pepper

3 tablespoons extra virgin olive oil

1 tablespoon sherry vinegar

6 thyme sprigs

1⅓lbs good-sized Brussels sprouts (any discolored outer leaves removed), trimmed and halved

1 large onion, cut into slim wedges

¼lb pancetta or slab bacon, cut into ½in chunks

¼lb cooked chestnuts

¼lb prunes, pitted and halved

5 tablespoons amontillado sherry

1 tablespoon maple syrup

1 tablespoon unsalted butter

ROASTED BROCCOLINI WITH CREAM & PARMESAN CHEESE

SERVES 4 AS A SIDE DISH,
OR AS PART OF A SPREAD
OF DISHES

1½lb broccolini

1½ tablespoons extra virgin
olive oil

sea salt flakes and freshly
ground black pepper

2 tablespoons unsalted
butter

¾ cup fresh white
breadcrumbs

1¼ cups heavy cream

generous ½ cup finely
grated Parmesan cheese,
or half Parmesan and half
Gruyère

I love roast broccolini served in all sorts of ways—with feta cheese and chopped preserved lemon scattered over, or with chopped fried anchovies, garlic, and chili—but this has all the deliciousness of a gratin without using quite as much cream. You could also add chopped anchovies and a finely grated garlic clove, or a couple of sautéed shallots, to the cream and pour this over the broccolini (there's no need to add the Parmesan cheese if you do this).

Preheat the oven to 400°F.

Trim the bottoms of the broccolini stalks. If any of the spears are thick, halve them along their length.

Put the broccolini in a roasting pan or on a sheet pan and toss with the olive oil and seasoning. Roast for 12 minutes.

Melt the butter in a frying pan. Add the breadcrumbs and turn them over until they are buttery, but not toasted.

Pour the cream over the broccolini, season, and sprinkle on the cheese and the buttered crumbs. Return to the oven and roast for a final 10–11 minutes, or until golden and bubbling. Serve immediately.

SALAD OF ROASTED CARROTS, APPLE & LENTILS WITH CHILI & PRESERVED LEMONS

I know this sounds odd, but it works, and it works as a main course lunch salad, not just as a supporting side dish. The real surprise of this recipe is just how good apples are with chilies and preserved lemons.

Preheat the oven to 400°F.

Trim the carrots, but leave a bit of green tuft. If you can't find young carrots, halve or quarter larger ones lengthwise. Don't peel them, just wash them well. Place in a single layer in a roasting pan. Add the olive oil, salt, and pepper, then toss to ensure the carrots are coated.

Roast in the oven for 30–35 minutes, or until tender. Be careful not to overcook them.

Make the dressing by putting the vinegar in a bowl and whisking in all the other ingredients with a fork. Season.

Put the lentils into a broad shallow serving bowl with half the chili and one-third of the preserved lemon. Season a little, then toss with about one-third of the dressing.

Halve and core the apple or apples (there's no need to peel them) and cut into matchsticks. Throw into a large mixing bowl with the lemon juice and add the carrots. Add the rest of the preserved lemons and chili, along with two-thirds of the herbs and the remaining dressing.

Throw the rest of the mint and cilantro into the lentils. Put the carrot and apple mixture on top—you should still be able to see the lentils around the sides—and serve.

SERVES 4 AS A SIDE DISH

FOR THE SALAD

¾lb young carrots (a mixture of colors is best, if you can find them)

3 tablespoons extra virgin olive oil

sea salt flakes and freshly ground black pepper

1¼ cups cooked Puy lentils

1 red Fresno chili and 1 green chili, halved, seeded, and very finely shredded

2 preserved lemons, rind only, finely shredded, plus 2 teaspoons brine from the jar

1 large or 2 medium tart apples

juice of ½ lemon

leaves from 10 mint sprigs, torn

¼ cup cilantro leaves

FOR THE DRESSING

2 tablespoons white balsamic vinegar

⅓ cup extra virgin olive oil (fruity rather than grassy)

1 fat garlic clove, finely grated

½in fresh ginger, peeled and finely grated

¼ teaspoon clear honey

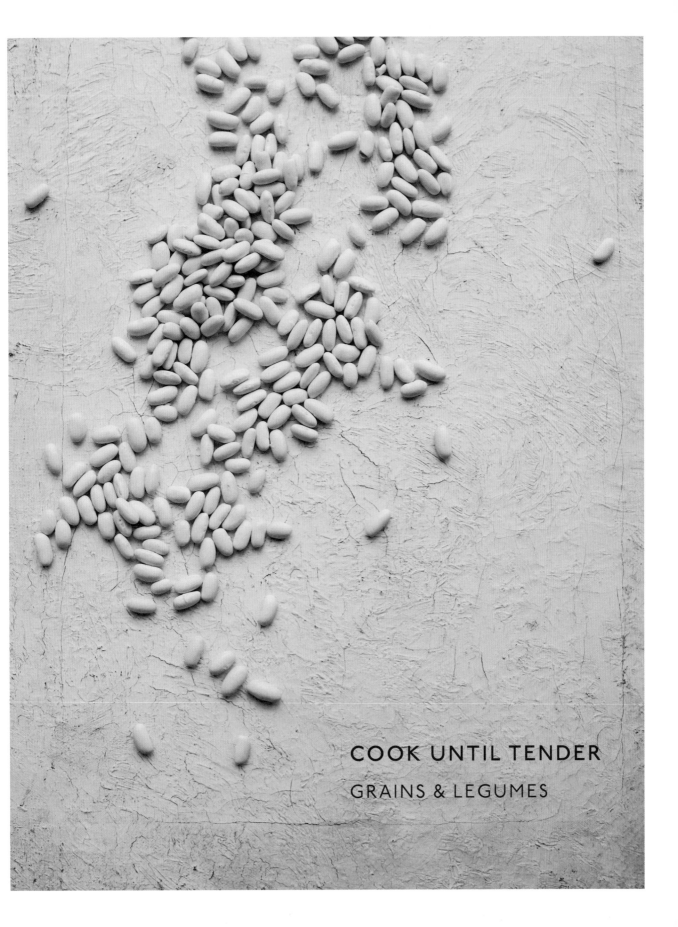

COOK UNTIL TENDER

GRAINS & LEGUMES

SAUSAGES & LENTILS
WITH HERB RELISH

Why bake the lentils for this, rather than cook them on the stovetop? Well, because they become imbued with the juices from the sausages and they keep their shape better, each lentil a perfect little lens. They also seem to taste much more intense than any pulses I cook on the stovetop. You have to use exactly the size of dish stipulated, so that the lentils—and the stock in which they're baking—cook at the right rate.

Preheat the oven to 375°F.

Heat the olive oil in an ovenproof sauté pan and brown the sausages all over (you just need to color them, not cook them through). Lift the sausages out. Add the onion, celery, carrot, and pancetta or bacon lardons to the pan and sauté until the bacon is golden. Separately mix the stock and wine or cider together in a measuring cup.

Add the garlic and lentils to the pan with the bay leaves and toss with the vegetables, then add 2¼ cups of the stock mixture. Bring to a boil, season, return the sausages, then transfer to the oven.

Cook, uncovered, for 15 minutes. Stir and add the rest of the stock mixture, then cover and bake for a final 25–30 minutes. The lentils should be tender and the liquid almost completely absorbed. Taste for seasoning, though the reduced stock, wine, and bacon should have made the dish quite salty enough.

Make the relish. Either chop the herbs and capers finely and mix with the other ingredients, or whizz everything together in a food processor. Taste for seasoning.

Serve the sausages and lentils with the relish. Serve Dijon mustard and crusty bread on the side.

SERVES 4

FOR THE SAUSAGES AND LENTILS

1½ tablespoons extra virgin olive oil

8 good-quality pork sausages

1 onion, finely chopped

½ celery stalk, finely chopped

1 medium carrot, finely chopped

¼lb pancetta or bacon lardons

2 cups chicken stock

1½ cups dry white wine or dry hard cider

1 garlic clove, finely grated

2⅓ cups Puy lentils

2 bay leaves

sea salt flakes and freshly ground black pepper

Dijon mustard and crusty bread, to serve

FOR THE RELISH

4 cups soft herb leaves such as flat-leaf parsley, basil, mint, chives, or a mix of whatever you have

1½ tablespoons capers, rinsed, drained, and patted dry

2 garlic cloves, very finely chopped

½ teaspoon Dijon mustard

juice of 1 lemon

7 tablespoons extra virgin olive oil

OVEN-BAKED BEANS WITH ROSEMARY & CHILI

SERVES 8

2½ cups dried cannellini or haricot beans

1 celery stalk, finely chopped

4 large rosemary sprigs

2 large carrots, halved lengthwise

1 large onion, quartered

2 heads of garlic, halved horizontally

¼ cup extra virgin olive oil

sea salt flakes and freshly ground black pepper

3½ tablespoons tomato paste

1 teaspoon crushed red pepper

handful of white breadcrumbs (optional)

You do have to start these beans on the stovetop—getting them to simmering point—before transferring them to the oven, but I much prefer them being baked behind that closed door. They keep their shape better and their flavor really intensifies. You might need to add liquid, depending on how soupy or how thick you want the end result to be. You can also thicken the beans simply by continuing to cook them without a lid, or by adding breadcrumbs.

Put the beans in a large bowl, cover with plenty of cold water, and leave to soak overnight.

The next day, preheat the oven to 300°F.

Drain the beans and put them into a large ovenproof saucepan with the celery, rosemary, carrots, onion, garlic, and olive oil. Add plenty of pepper and enough water to cover the beans by about 1½in. Bring to a boil on the stovetop, then transfer, uncovered, to the oven. Bake for 1 hour, checking every so often to see that the beans are moist.

Now you can remove the carrots if you want to. I usually leave one in and chop it roughly with a knife (just in the pot) and remove the other. The chopped one eventually disintegrates and helps the sauce around the beans to thicken, but not everyone likes the sweetness of the carrot and you might prefer the dish to taste more purely of beans.

Add the tomato paste, crushed red pepper, and some salt to the saucepan and stir. Return the pot to the oven, again uncovered, and cook for a final hour. The top will become glossy and thick and almost slightly dry. When that happens, stir the beans: that skin forming on the top is delicious and you want to distribute it. You can cook the beans until they are as thick as you want them, or you can add breadcrumbs for the last 10 minutes of cooking to thicken the beans (if you do add breadcrumbs, adjust the seasoning again, as the dish may need more salt).

BAKED BABY PUMPKINS STUFFED WITH WILD MUSHROOMS, SCALLIONS, GRAINS & GRUYÉRE CHEESE

This is the kind of dish that can be a bit of a hassle by the time you've sautéed and roasted the various components, so I've tried to simplify it. You can cook the grains yourself, of course (lentils are also good), but I often use pre-cooked packs. When small pumpkins aren't in season, bigger ones are fine, they just take more time to become tender before you add the stuffing.

Preheat the oven to 400°F. Cut the tops off the pumpkins so that each has a "lid," then remove the seeds and fibers from inside with a spoon. Rub the butter inside and season the insides, too, with salt, pepper, and nutmeg. Put in a roasting pan—along with the "lids"—and bake for 15 minutes, or until the flesh is soft when pierced with a knife.

Put the dried mushrooms into a bowl and add just enough boiling water to cover. Leave these to plump up for 20 minutes. Arrange the cremini mushrooms in a roasting pan or on a sheet pan in a single layer. It will look like a lot, but they shrink. Toss with 3 tablespoons of olive oil, season, and roast for 30 minutes. Mushrooms throw out a lot of liquid, but it will evaporate, and they should become quite dark. Put the scallions in another roasting pan in 1 layer, toss with the remaining 1½ tablespoons of oil, season, and roast alongside the mushrooms for 10–15 minutes. They should be tender. Cut them into 1¼in lengths.

Stir the grains, scallions, roast mushrooms, and dried mushrooms together, adding the mushroom soaking liquid. Add the thyme, garlic, and two-thirds of the cheese. Taste for seasoning. You can prepare the recipe up to this point in advance, then assemble and finish cooking it at the last minute.

Fill the pumpkins with the stuffing. Drizzle the cream into each and scatter on the remaining cheese. Bake for 10 minutes, or until they are soft and the cheesy tops are golden. Serve with the "lids" on.

SERVES 8

8 little pumpkins, 4–4½in in diameter

7 tablespoons unsalted butter, slightly softened

sea salt flakes and freshly ground black pepper

freshly grated nutmeg

1oz dried wild mushrooms

1lb 2oz cremini mushrooms, trimmed and halved

4½ tablespoons extra virgin olive oil

12 scallions, trimmed

scant 2 cups cooked grains (farro, barley or freekeh)

leaves from 2 thyme sprigs

1 garlic clove, finely grated

¼lb grated Gruyère cheese (sharp aged Cheddar and Fontina also work)

1 cup heavy cream

WHITE BEANS & ROASTED TOMATOES WITH CAPER, MINT & CHILI DRESSING

This is what I make when I have a load of cherry tomatoes that are slightly sagging—or a bit insipid—and need to be rescued. The oven condenses their sweetness.

Preheat the oven to 400°F.

Make a dressing by mixing the mustard with the white balsamic vinegar and some salt and pepper, then, using a fork, whisk in 5 tablespoons of the olive oil. Add the chili and garlic. Toss half of this in with the beans in a serving dish and leave to soak.

Put the cherry tomatoes in a roasting pan, drizzle with the remaining 2 tablespoons of oil, season, and roast for 15 minutes. Let cool a little.

If you're using mint or basil, just tear the leaves. If you're using parsley, chop it finely. Toss a little of this into the remaining dressing and add the rest of the herbs to the beans, along with the capers.

Lay the tomatoes on top of the beans, pouring on all their cooking juices, spoon over the remaining dressing, and serve.

smidgen of Dijon mustard (about ¼ teaspoon or less)

1¼ tablespoons white balsamic vinegar

sea salt flakes and freshly ground black pepper

7 tablespoons extra virgin olive oil

1 red Fresno chili, halved, seeded, and finely chopped, or a good pinch of crushed red pepper

1 small garlic clove, finely grated

15 oz can of cannellini beans, rinsed and left to drain and dry a little in a sieve

1lb 2oz cherry tomatoes

handful of mint, basil or flat-leaf parsley leaves, or any soft herb leaves you have

1¼ tablespoons capers, rinsed, drained, and patted dry

GRAINS ON THE SIDE...

Not every dish in this book has a starch incorporated into it, and I don't stretch my love of the oven to using it to cook foods that are better dealt with in another way (though there is a baked rice dish on page 156 that you can adapt at will). Here is a simple guide to cooking grains on the stovetop. Once drained, they can be mixed with melted butter or olive oil, herbs such as rosemary or thyme, nuts, crumbled cheese such as feta, or soaked and drained dried fruits.

WHITE LONG-GRAIN RICE Put the rice in a pan, add water so it covers it by 1in water (for me that is about a third of my index finger, which is a good way to judge it), and bring to a boil. Cook at a full boil until the water looks as if it has been absorbed and the surface of the rice is "pitted" with little holes. Cover the pan, place it over the lowest heat, and cook for 15–20 minutes (check after 15 minutes, lifting a few grains with a fork). It's important that you don't stir the rice until it's ready. Fork it through to aerate it before serving.

You can also cook rice in stock, which gives a much more intensely flavoured dish. Rinse the rice in a sieve until the water runs clear, then sauté a chopped onion in oil or butter until pale gold and soft. Stir in the rice, turning to coat in the fat, then pour in stock (1½ cups for every 1 cup rice) and bring to a boil, uncovered. Now continue as above. You can flavor this with spices, garlic, hard herbs, or citrus zest. If you're using spices and garlic, cook them for a few minutes once the onion is soft before adding the rice.

BROWN LONG-GRAIN RICE & CAMARGUE RED RICE Brown rice never softens the way white rice does, but retains a firm, nutty center. Cook it in boiling water for about 25 minutes, then drain. Camargue red rice cooks in the same way, though it only takes 20–25 minutes, and has the same chewy texture and a similar flavor.

WILD RICE Wild rice is from a native American water grass. It's best mixed with another grain, because of its texture (on its own it is very chewy), and because it looks striking. Simmer it on its own—it turns the water purple-grey—for 35 minutes.

COUSCOUS Couscous isn't a grain, but a grain product made from rolled semolina. You can now buy a whole wheat version, as well as couscous made from barley or kamut. Just pour boiling water or stock over the grains—¾ cup of liquid to 1 cup of couscous—cover with plastic wrap, and leave for 15 minutes. Finish with melted butter or olive oil and seasoning and fork it through to aerate it.

BULGUR WHEAT Quicker and easier than rice and gloriously nutty. It's made when wheat (usually durum) is boiled, dried, cracked, then sorted by size. Cook in boiling water or stock. The time it takes depends on the coarseness of the grain, so check after 10 minutes (medium cooks in 15 minutes), then fork it through to aerate it, cover, and leave to stand for another 5 minutes. I generally cook it in stock, using twice the volume of liquid to grain.

FARRO & SPELT Farro is emmer wheat, a really old grain. The type most commonly available is semi-pearled (labeled *semi-perlato*). It doesn't need soaking and cooks in 20–25 minutes. The unpearled type, should you find it, needs to be soaked overnight and takes an hour to cook (it's quite like hulled barley in both taste and appearance). Spelt is also an ancient wheat grain, and the two are often used interchangeably. Cook spelt just like semi-pearled farro.

FREEKEH This is roasted young green wheat, cooked mostly in the Middle East. It has a good assertive flavor—smoky and nutty—and a firm texture. Boil it in water for 20–25 minutes, then drain.

BARLEY Pearl barley is the type most commonly available. This has been processed: the germ and some of the bran has been removed. The unprocessed type, hulled barley, takes about an hour to cook (and needs to be soaked overnight beforehand). Pearl barley cooks in 25–30 minutes.

QUINOA This is often cooked with too much liquid, so you end up with something like gruel. Use a scant 3 cups water or stock for every 2 cups quinoa and cook gently—simmer, don't boil—for 15 minutes. It also helps the flavor if you toast the quinoa in a dry frying pan before you cook it.

BAKED BEANS WITH SMOKED BACON, PORK BELLY & MOLASSES

This is based on an American classic, Boston Baked Beans, but it contains a bit more meat than the original. I love the smokiness, but you can use unsmoked bacon if you prefer. This can be easily reheated… in fact, it tastes even better the next day.

Put the beans in a bowl, cover with plenty of water, and soak overnight.

Preheat the oven to 300°F.

Drain the beans. Put them in a large ovenproof saucepan or casserole with the celery, half the rosemary, the carrots, and the quartered onion. Add plenty of pepper and enough water to cover by about 1¼in. Bring to a boil, cover, and transfer to the oven. Bake for 1 hour.

Remove the carrots and celery. I usually just leave the onion, but fish it out if you want. Add the rest of the rosemary, the chopped onion, and the garlic.

Heat the olive oil in a frying pan over medium heat and brown the bacon and pork. Add these to the bean saucepan. Stir in the molasses, mustard, sugar, tomato paste, and crushed red pepper and season well. Bring to a boil once more, then return to the oven, this time leaving it uncovered.

Bake for 3 hours—you might even need a bit longer—gently turning the beans over a couple of times during the cooking time and keeping an eye on the level of the liquid. You want the juices to reduce so that you are left with a thick mass, but you don't want the beans to get too dry. When they have 1 hour of cooking time left, add the cider vinegar, to cut the sweetness and add depth to the flavor. In the last hour of cooking, it's best to leave the beans alone, so they get a lovely baked crust on top.

Serve in warmed broad, flat soup plates or pasta bowls. You don't need anything starchy with this—and the dish is usually served on its own—but I do like cabbage with it.

SERVES 8

2½ cups dried beans, such as cannellini, borlotti ,or pinto

1 celery stalk

4 large rosemary sprigs

2 large carrots, halved lengthwise

2 large onions, 1 quartered, 1 chopped

sea salt flakes and freshly ground black pepper

2 heads of garlic, halved horizontally

1 tablespoon extra virgin olive oil

7oz smoked slab bacon in 1 piece, cut into ½-inch chunks

1lb boneless pork belly, rind removed, cut into 1in-thick slices and halved

2 tablespoons light molasses

2 tablespoons Dijon mustard

3 tablespoons light brown sugar

2 tablespoons tomato paste

1–2 teaspoons crushed red pepper, depending how spicy you want it

1–2 tablespoons cider vinegar, or to taste

steamed cabbage, to serve (optional)

SOUTH AMERICAN-SPICED CHICKEN, BLACK BEANS, & RICE WITH AVOCADO, PICKLED CHILIES & SOUR CREAM

Another baked rice dish, so again you do need to cook it in the size of pan specified. The chicken, beans, and rice are, in themselves, simple, but it's the add-ons here that make the dish.

Preheat the oven to 375°F.

Heat the oil in a 12in ovenproof sauté pan or shallow casserole (the size is very important) and quickly brown the chicken pieces on both sides, just to give them a good color. Remove and set aside. Add the onion and peppers to the pan and sauté for 5 minutes, or until just starting to soften.

Add the garlic, cumin, cinnamon, and chilies and cook for about 2 minutes, then add the black beans and cherry tomatoes. Sprinkle on the rice (it's important that the black beans are underneath the rice and chicken when the dish goes into the oven, otherwise they get scorched). Pour on the boiling stock and return the chicken to the pan, skin side up. Season.

Bake for 40 minutes. The chicken should be lovely and golden and the stock should have been absorbed. The rice should be tender by this time, too. Sprinkle on the cilantro.

Serve with lime wedges, a bowl of pickled chilies, sour cream, and slices of avocado (just squeeze lime juice over the avocados in a bowl and sprinkle with salt and pepper).

SERVES 4

FOR THE CHICKEN, BEANS AND RICE

2 tablespoons extra virgin olive oil or peanut oil

8 good-sized skin-on, bone-in chicken thighs, or a mixture of chicken parts, excess skin neatly trimmed

1 large onion, roughly chopped

2 bell peppers, halved, seeded, and sliced

3 garlic cloves, finely grated

1 teaspoon ground cumin

1 cinnamon stick, halved

2 red Fresno chilies, halved, seeded, and chopped

15oz can of black beans, drained and rinsed

⅓lb cherry tomatoes, halved

1 cup basmati rice, washed in a sieve until the water runs clear

2½ cups boiling chicken stock

sea salt flakes and freshly ground black pepper

3 tablespoons chopped cilantro leaves

TO SERVE

lime wedges

pickled chilies

sour cream

2 avocados

BAKED RICE WITH GREEN OLIVES, ORANGE, FETA CHEESE & DILL

A blueprint for baked rice. Just stick to the same quantities of rice and liquid, the same size of pan, and the same oven temperature and you can produce endless variations. Change the herbs, use spices, or add nuts and dried fruit.

Preheat the oven to 400°F.

Put the rice in a sieve and run cold water through it until the water runs clear to remove the excess starch, then leave it in the sieve to drain.

In a 12in ovenproof sauté pan or shallow casserole, heat the olive oil and sauté the onions over medium-low heat until they're soft and pale gold. Add the garlic and cumin and cook for another 2 minutes, then add the rinsed and drained rice, the orange juice, and the boiling stock. Season.

Bring to a boil on the stovetop, then transfer immediately to the oven. Bake, uncovered, for 1 hour.

When there are 10 minutes to go, break up the crust that has formed on the top and stir in the olives. By the end of cooking time, the rice should be tender and all the stock absorbed.

Scatter the orange zest, feta, and dill over the top, drizzle with olive oil, and serve. You will find that the rice has formed a delicious crust on the bottom of the pan.

1¾ cups basmati rice

3 tablespoons extra virgin olive oil, plus more to serve

2 large onions, roughly chopped

4 garlic cloves, crushed

1 tablespoon ground cumin

finely grated zest and juice of 1 orange

3½ cups boiling chicken or vegetable stock

sea salt flakes and freshly ground black pepper

½ cup good-quality green olives, preferably pitted, roughly chopped or left whole

1 cup crumbled feta cheese

½ cup roughly chopped dill

ARROZ AL HORNO

*Muscular and comforting, this is brilliant for a cold night.
It also feeds eight with very little effort. You do need to use a pan
12–13½in in diameter, so the rice cooks at the right rate. Unlike
risottos, paellas shouldn't be stirred, which means they're pretty
low effort to make.*

Preheat the oven to 375°F.

Heat the olive oil in a deep ovenproof frying or sauté pan, or shallow casserole, about 12in in diameter, or a little bigger. Over a high heat, brown the pork belly slices on both sides, then lift them out into a bowl.

Reduce the heat to medium, put the chorizo and bacon in the pan, and sauté all over, then remove with a slotted spoon and set aside with the pork.

Fry the onion and peppers in the fat remaining in the pan until soft and pale gold, then add the tomato and cook until that is soft, too. Add the garlic, smoked paprika, and crushed red pepper, if using, and cook for another 2 minutes, then return the pork, chorizo, and bacon to the pan. Add the beans, whichever herb you're using, and the stock and bring everything to a boil.

Sprinkle the rice around the bits of pork, pushing it below the level of the stock. Return to a boil, season well, then transfer—uncovered—to the oven.

Cook for 30 minutes, without stirring, then check to see how it's doing. The rice should be tender and the stock absorbed. If it's not ready, return it to the oven for another 5 minutes, then check again. Taste for seasoning and adjust it if necessary.

Squeeze lemon juice over the top and drizzle on some extra virgin olive oil if you want.

SERVES 8

1 tablespoon extra virgin olive oil, plus more to serve (optional)

1¾lbs 1in-thick boneless pork belly slices (about 4), halved

⅓lb Spanish cooking chorizo, chopped

¼lb ½-inch unsmoked bacon lardons

1 onion, finely chopped

2 red bell peppers, halved, seeded, and sliced

1 plum tomato, chopped

8 garlic cloves, roughly chopped

4 teaspoons smoked paprika

½ teaspoon crushed red pepper (optional)

½ x 14oz can of white beans, drained and rinsed (haricot, cannellini, or butter beans are all fine)

6 thyme or rosemary sprigs

4 cups chicken stock

1¾ cups paella rice

sea salt flakes and freshly ground black pepper

lemon juice, to serve (optional)

ARROZ CON VERDURAS

You can use any vegetables you like here—tomatoes, pumpkin, eggplants, zucchini, white beans, whatever is in season—just make sure that anything that takes a long time to cook is cut small enough to be ready in the time the dish is in the oven. Conversely, quick-cooking vegetables such as broccolini or asparagus should be added to the dish later on. This is quite spicy; if you want a milder version, reduce the quantities of smoked paprika and chili. Allioli—garlic mayonnaise—is lovely with this, if you can be bothered to make it (see page 198).

Preheat the oven to 400°F.

Heat 2 tablespoons of the olive oil in a shallow casserole or a large ovenproof sauté pan, or a paella pan measuring around 12in in diameter (a little bigger or smaller is OK).

Fry the onion and peppers until soft and pale gold, then add the tomatoes and cook until they are soft, too, and the mixture is thick and sloppy.

Add the garlic, smoked paprika, and crushed red pepper and cook for 2 minutes. Stir in the chickpeas, thyme, stock, and saffron (if you're using it) and bring to a boil. Sprinkle the rice on top and lay the pumpkin slices in the pan.

Season well and transfer the dish to the oven, uncovered. Cook for 25 minutes without stirring, then check to see how the rice is doing. It should be almost tender and the stock nearly absorbed. If the stock has already been absorbed and there is a danger of the rice drying out, pour in a little more.

Toss the broccolini in the remaining 1 tablespoon oil, season, and scatter it over the top. Return to the oven for a final 10 minutes.

Squeeze some lemon juice over the dish, if you like, and serve, drizzled with some extra virgin olive oil if you like.

SERVES 6–8

3 tablespoons extra virgin olive oil, plus more to serve (optional)

1 large onion, finely chopped

3 red bell peppers, halved, seeded, and sliced

6 plum tomatoes, chopped

8 garlic cloves, roughly chopped

5 teaspoons smoked paprika, or less, if you prefer

½ teaspoon crushed red pepper

14oz can of chickpeas, drained and rinsed

6 thyme sprigs

6⅔ cups vegetable stock, plus more if needed

generous pinch of saffron threads (optional)

1½ cups paella rice

1⅓lbs pumpkin or winter squash, seeds and fibers removed, cut into wedges

sea salt flakes and freshly ground black pepper

¼lb broccolini, any thicker stems halved lengthwise

lemon juice, to serve (optional)

CHICKEN & RICE WITH COCONUT, GREEN CHILIES, CILANTRO & LIME

SERVES 4–6

1 tablespoon peanut oil

8 good-sized skin-on, bone-in chicken thighs, excess skin neatly trimmed

1 large onion, roughly chopped

4 garlic cloves, finely grated

1¼in fresh ginger, peeled and finely grated

2 teaspoons ground coriander

2 teaspoons ground cumin

2 green chilies, halved, seeded, and finely chopped

½lb butternut squash, peeled, seeded, and sliced (prepared weight)

¼lb cauliflower florets

1½ cups basmati rice

½ cup chopped cilantro leaves

finely grated zest and juice of 2 limes

2 Makrut lime leaves

sea salt flakes and freshly ground black pepper

1¼ cups coconut milk

1⅔ cups chicken stock

chutney and plain yogurt, to serve (optional)

Easy one-dish cooking. Leave the seeds of one of the chilies intact if you prefer things hotter. You can use just a single vegetable (cauliflower or squash) instead of both, if you like. You don't have to serve any more vegetables on the side, but some chutney and yogurt would be good.

Preheat the oven to 375°F.

Heat the oil in a shallow casserole or sauté pan 12in in diameter, and quickly fry the chicken thighs just to get some color on them (they will darken further in the oven). Put them on a plate.

Sauté the onion in the pan until it's soft and pale gold. Add the garlic, ginger, spices, and chilies and cook for 2 minutes, then stir in the squash and cauliflower. Tip in the rice, half the cilantro, the lime zest, half the lime juice, the lime leaves, and seasoning. Return the chicken to the pan skin side up, along with any juices that have run from it. Season the top of the chicken.

Heat the coconut milk and chicken stock in a saucepan until just under boiling. Pour this around the chicken thighs and put the pan into the oven, uncovered. Cook for 35 minutes. The chicken should be cooked through and the liquid should have been absorbed by the rice.

Squeeze the remaining lime juice over the top and scatter with the rest of the cilantro. Serve immediately, with chutney and yogurt, if you like.

CHICKEN WITH WILD MUSHROOMS, PUMPKIN, RICE & SAGE BUTTER

If the butter is an effort too far, leave it out—it's still a good dish. This is also lovely with a generous handful of grated Parmesan or pecorino cheese sprinkled on top 15 minutes before the end of the cooking time. You don't have to use only chicken thighs, you can use a mixture of thighs and drumsticks if you prefer.

Preheat the oven to 400°F.

Soak the wild mushrooms in ⅓ cup just-boiled water for 15 minutes.

To make the sage butter, mash the butter with the sage and garlic and set it aside (I only chill this if I'm going to keep it for a while).

Drain the wild mushrooms, adding their soaking liquid to the chicken stock.

Wash the rice in a sieve under the cold tap, until the water runs clear, to remove the excess starch.

Put the onion and both the cremini and dried mushrooms into a 12in sauté pan or shallow casserole (the width is very important) and sprinkle on the rice (it may not look like much, but it expands, don't worry). Put the chicken thighs, skin side up, and the pumpkin on top. Sprinkle a little olive oil over the vegetables and chicken and season well. Bring the stock mixture to a boil, then carefully pour it around the chicken thighs.

Bake in the oven for 45 minutes, by which time the chicken will be lovely and golden and the stock will have been absorbed. Put pats of the sage butter over the chicken thighs, allow it to melt, then serve.

SERVES 4

FOR THE CHICKEN AND RICE

½oz dried wild mushrooms

2 cups chicken stock

1 cup basmati rice

1 onion, roughly chopped

¼lb cremini mushrooms, trimmed and thickly sliced

8 good-sized skin-on, bone-in chicken thighs, excess skin neatly trimmed

¾lb pumpkin or butternut squash, seeded, and chopped into big chunks or wedges (prepared weight)

a little extra virgin olive oil

sea salt flakes and freshly ground black pepper

FOR THE SAGE BUTTER

5 tablespoons unsalted butter, at room temperature

6 sage leaves, finely chopped

1 small garlic clove, finely grated

WEEKENDS & HOLIDAYS

ROASTS, BIRDS, & WHOLE FISH

HOT & SWEET GINGER POUSSINS

Sticky, messy, quick. If you can't find poussins, Cornish game hens split into two equal halves (use kitchen scissors to cut out the backbone, then use a heavy knife to slice through the breastbone) will also work here. In the summer, a cucumber salad is good alongside (see page 184); in the winter, stir-fried bok choy. Provide plenty of paper napkins.

Put the *kecap manis*, soy sauce, and fish sauce in a saucepan with the sugar. Heat gently, stirring to help the sugar dissolve. Leave to cool, then add the lime juice, sriracha, garlic, and ginger.

Put the poussins in a dish and add the marinade, making sure it goes inside the birds' cavities as well as over the outsides. Cover the dish with plastic wrap and put in the refrigerator, preferably overnight, but even for a couple of hours is good. Turn the birds over in the marinade every so often. When you're ready to cook, bring the birds to room temperature.

Preheat the oven to 375°F.

Put the poussins into a roasting pan—or 2 roasting pans if yours are small—and roast for 50 minutes (or 35-40 minutes if using Cornish game hens).

Pour the marinade left behind into a small saucepan and bring to a boil, then remove from the heat. Use this to baste the poussins as they cook (it's very important to reheat the marinade to the boiling point, so it's safe for you to use it to baste the partly-cooked birds).

You might have to cover the birds with foil towards the end of the cooking time. They'll become a lovely dark mahogany color, but you don't want them to burn. To test for doneness, check that the juices that run from between the body of a bird and the leg when it is pierced are clear, with no trace of pink.

Serve the poussins brushed with a final layer of the marinade and sprinkled with sesame seeds. These are good with boiled rice, a stir-fried green vegetable such as bok choy, and lime wedges.

SERVES 6

FOR THE POUSSINS

1 cup *kecap manis* (Indonesian sweet soy sauce)

½ cup light soy sauce

½ cup fish sauce

¾ cup light brown sugar

juice of 2 limes

2 tablespoons sriracha, plus more if you want the poussins to be hotter

4 garlic cloves, finely grated

1½in fresh ginger, peeled and finely grated

6 poussins, or 3 Cornish game hens split into equal halves

TO SERVE

sesame seeds

boiled rice

stir-fried green vegetables

lime wedges

SALMON ROASTED IN BUTTER WITH BEET & HORSERADISH PURÉE

*A whole salmon can seem like a real number—we mess around
with fish poachers and the like—and, even when roasted, it is
a big thing to eat your way through. A side of salmon cooked in
butter, however, is less expensive and serves a smaller number of
people, but still has impact. If you don't like beets, serve another
sauce; a mixture of mayonnaise and fromage blanc with chopped
herbs, capers, and shallots is good, or check the endless list of
possible embellishments (see pages 206–207).*

Preheat the oven to 450°F.

For the purée, put everything except the crème fraîche into a food processor,
season, and whizz until smooth. Scrape this into a bowl and add the crème
fraîche. Taste for seasoning. You might need to adjust the lemon juice and
vinegar, too.

Find a heavy roasting pan big enough to hold the salmon. Run your hand over
the surface of the fish from head to tail to make sure that there are no bones;
if there are, remove them with your fingers. Season the fish.

Melt the butter in the roasting pan over medium-low heat on the stovetop,
then add half the herbs and put the salmon on top, skin side up. Transfer to
the oven and roast for 5 minutes. Remove from the oven and take the skin
off—it should peel off quite easily—then season the flesh and flip the salmon
over. Sprinkle with the remaining herbs and return to the oven for a final
6–8 minutes. Carefully slide the point of a sharp knife into the thickest
part of the fish: it should be opaque, not translucent.

Serve on a warmed platter with dill (or chervil) sprigs and lemon wedges.
Offer the beet and horseradish purée on the side.

SERVES 6

FOR THE PURÉE

1lb cooked beets (not
pickled)

1 small garlic clove,
finely grated

juice of ½ lemon, or
to taste

1 tablespoon white balsamic
vinegar, or to taste

1 tablespoon peeled
and finely grated fresh
horseradish

1 tablespoon crème fraîche

sea salt flakes and freshly
ground black pepper

FOR THE FISH

2¼lbs salmon fillet,
pin-bones removed

3 tablespoons unsalted
butter

3 tablespoons equal parts
chopped flat-leaf parsley
and dill leaves (chervil is also
fantastic, if you can find it or
you grow it), plus dill sprigs
to serve

lemon wedges, to serve

ROASTED LEG OF LAMB WITH BASIL, PECORINO, GARLIC & WINE

This came about after I cooked a Greek dish that had a stuffing made from a Greek cheese (not unlike pecorino) and ground allspice. I'd never thought about a cheese stuffing for lamb before. So this is just something that came out of my kitchen for Sunday lunch one week: Italian ingredients, Greek-inspired.

Preheat the oven to 450°F.

Put the cheese, garlic, and some salt into a mortar and pound to a rough purée, gradually adding the olive oil. Tear the basil leaves, add them to the mortar, and pound them, too.

Place the leg of lamb in a roasting pan. Make deep incisions all over it and push the paste from the mortar down into them. You can also loosen the meat around the bone to make a pocket and push the paste into that, too. Season all over and put into the oven.

Roast for 15 minutes, then reduce the oven temperature to 375°F. Add the onions, potatoes, and tomatoes to the roasting pan, toss them in the fat in the pan, adding a little more oil if it's needed to moisten them, then season and roast for a final 45 minutes, adding the wine after 20 minutes. The lamb will be pink. If you prefer it more well done, cook it for a little longer.

Remove the lamb to a plate, cover with foil, insulate well (I use old towels or tea towels), and leave to rest for 15 minutes. If the potatoes are tender, cover them and keep warm in a low oven while the lamb rests; if they're still a bit firm, increase the oven temperature to 400°F, return the vegetables to the oven, uncovered, and cook until they're ready.

Serve the lamb with the potatoes, tomatoes, and onions, scattered with a few basil leaves, if you like.

SERVES 6–8

2¼ cups finely grated pecorino cheese

6 garlic cloves, finely grated

sea salt flakes and freshly ground black pepper

3 tablespoons extra virgin olive oil, plus more if needed

⅓ cup basil leaves, plus more to serve (optional)

4lb leg of lamb

2 medium red onions, cut into wedges

1⅓lb small waxy potatoes, scrubbed, then halved or quartered, depending on size

¾lb red and yellow cherry tomatoes, halved or quartered

generous 1 cup white wine

PERSIAN-SPICED SPATCHCOCKED CHICKEN WITH QUICK-PICKLED RED ONIONS & DILL YOGURT

SERVES 6

FOR THE SPICE MIX

1 tablespoon black peppercorns

1 teaspoon coriander seeds

seeds from 8 cardamom pods

1 tablespoon edible dried rose petals (optional)

½ teaspoon freshly grated nutmeg

¾ teaspoon ground turmeric

FOR THE CHICKEN

4lb whole chicken

5 garlic cloves, finely grated

2 tablespoons extra virgin olive oil, plus more to rub

sea salt flakes and freshly ground black pepper

1¼ cups Greek yogurt

small bunch of dill, leaves chopped, any thicker stalks discarded

rice or bulgur wheat, to serve

FOR THE QUICK-PICKLED ONIONS

½ cup white wine vinegar

3 tablespoons granulated sugar

1 red onion, thinly sliced

The recipe for the spice mix here makes more than you need, but keep it for next time. You can leave out the pickled red onions if you want, but the spice mix is quite aromatic, so they bring a good tart-sweet contrast.

To make the spice mix, put the peppercorns, coriander seeds, cardamom seeds, and rose petals, if using, into a mortar and bash until roughly ground. Add the nutmeg and turmeric.

Spatchcock the chicken (it's easy, *see* page 198). Put it in a large roasting pan.

Mix 4 of the grated garlic cloves with the 2 tablespoons olive oil and some seasoning. Carefully lift the skin on the chicken breast without tearing it, and loosen it so that you can push the garlic and oil paste over the breast. If you can lift the skin enough, push it over the legs, too.

Rub 1 tablespoon of the spice mix all over the bird and season. Smear with olive oil and rub that in, too. Cover and put it into the refrigerator to marinate for up to 6 hours, or you can roast it right away. If you're cooking it now, preheat the oven to 400°F. Roast for 1 hour.

For the quick-pickled onions, heat the vinegar with 5 tablespoons of water, the sugar, and a pinch of sea salt flakes until the sugar and salt dissolve. Add the onion and remove from the heat. Leave to sit for 1 hour (longer is fine).

Stir the reserved grated garlic clove into the yogurt with the dill. Serve the chicken with the pickled onions, yogurt, and a bowl of rice or bulgur wheat.

STUFFED GREEK CHICKEN WITH CAYENNE, OREGANO & ORZO

SERVES 6

4lb whole chicken

½ cup crumbled feta cheese

¼lb tomatoes, chopped

1 cup crusty sourdough bread, torn into small pieces

4 tablespoons extra virgin olive oil, plus more to drizzle

2 garlic cloves, finely grated

3 teaspoons dried oregano

sea salt flakes and freshly ground black pepper

½ teaspoon cayenne pepper

1¼ cups orzo

2 cups boiling chicken stock

1 tablespoon chopped flat-leaf parsley leaves, or chopped leaves from 4 oregano sprigs

salad greens or roasted bell peppers, to serve

The perfect recipe for a spring Sunday lunch, with everything you need all in one dish. You have double carbs—orzo and stuffing— but it works: the bread becomes deliciously soft and soggy with the juices from the tomatoes. Try serving it with Roast Radishes with Honey, Mint & Preserved Lemon (see page 73), open some rosé, and contemplate the approaching summer.

Preheat the oven to 400°F.

Put the chicken into an ovenproof dish—I use a cast-iron one—which is 12in in diameter. Mix the feta, tomatoes, bread, olive oil, garlic, half the dried oregano, and some seasoning in a bowl. Stuff this into the chicken cavity.

Rub the chicken—breast and legs—with the cayenne, sprinkle with the rest of the dried oregano, then season the bird and drizzle it with olive oil.

Roast in the oven for 50 minutes.

Sprinkle the orzo around the chicken and pour on the boiling stock. Return to the oven for a final 20 minutes. Check during this time to make sure the orzo isn't becoming dry: there should be enough stock in it, but top it up with a little boiling water if you need to.

The chicken should be cooked: check by piercing it deeply between the leg and the body, the juices that run out should be clear, with no traces of pink. The orzo should be tender and the stock should have been absorbed.

Stir the fresh chopped herbs into the orzo and serve the chicken right from the dish. Salad greens or roasted red peppers is all you need on the side.

ROAST PORK WITH CRUSHED GRAPES, MARSALA & JUNIPER

SERVES 6

4lb boned pork
loin, rolled and tied

6 garlic cloves, cut into
fine slivers

½ tablespoon sea salt flakes

½ tablespoon black
peppercorns

leaves from 3 rosemary
sprigs

1 tablespoon juniper berries

2 tablespoons extra virgin
olive oil

1lb 2oz black seedless grapes

1½ cups dry Marsala

I don't cook roast pork that often—I just didn't grow up with it, we were a lamb- and chicken-eating family—but when I do, it's usually with fruit. This is gorgeously autumnal.

Unroll the pork and lay it on a board, flesh side up. Make incisions all over the meat with a sharp knife, then push the slivers of garlic into the incisions.

Crush the salt, peppercorns, rosemary leaves, and juniper berries roughly in a mortar, then stir in the olive oil.

Rub the seasoning mix into the pork, again on the flesh side, pushing bits inside the incisions. Put the pork in a dish, cover, and refrigerate overnight.

The next day, remove the pork from the refrigerator and allow it to come to room temperature. Preheat the oven to 400°F.

Roll the loin firmly, keeping as much of the seasoning inside as you can, then tie it at intervals with kitchen string. Put it in a heavy roasting pan and season all over. Roast for 25 minutes, then reduce the oven temperature to 375°F.

Pull half the grapes from their stems, cut the rest of the bunch into sprigs, and add them all to the roasting pan with 1 cup of the Marsala. Continue roasting for 60 minutes. Test the meat for doneness: the juices should run clear when the flesh is pierced to the center with a metal skewer.

Remove the pork from the pan, along with the grapes that are on sprigs, and put them on a warmed serving platter. Cover and allow to rest for 15 minutes.

Set the roasting pan over medium heat, add the remaining Marsala, and crush the loose grapes into the juices. Boil until you have a slightly syrupy mixture. Serve the pork with the Marsala sauce and the sprigs of roasted grapes.

ROAST BEEF TENDERLOIN WITH CRIMSON LEAVES, BUTTERMILK, WALNUTS & CASHEL BLUE CHEESE

A very expensive dish, I know, but this is the kind of thing to serve on festive occasions such as Thanksgiving, Christmas, or New Year's. It's particularly good on those days that aren't weighed down by a traditional dish (basically, when you don't have to serve a turkey), but you want something luxurious and generous. I wouldn't serve a roasted vegetable as well, just some boiled little waxy potatoes or good bread.

Preheat the oven to 425°F.

Bring the meat to room temperature. Season the beef really well all over and heat the oil or beef fat in a large frying pan. When the fat is smoking, add the beef and brown it on all sides. Transfer the roas to a roasting pan and roast for 10 minutes, then reduce the oven temperature to 400°F) and cook for another 20 minutes. Cover the meat with foil, insulate it with kitchen towels or old towels, and leave it to rest for 15 minutes.

To make the dressing, put the buttermilk, sour cream, olive oil, white balsamic vinegar, mustard, garlic, and seasoning into a bowl and mix with a fork. Taste for seasoning.

Put the greens—tear the larger ones—into a broad, shallow bowl or onto a platter and throw on the walnuts and the cheese. Drizzle or spoon the dressing over the top (don't drown the leaves, just serve the extra dressing on the side).

Slice the beef and serve it with the greens, cheese, and dressing.

SERVES 8

FOR THE BEEF
4lb beef tenderloin

sea salt flakes and freshly ground black pepper

1 tablespoon peanut oil, olive oil, or beef fat

FOR THE SALAD
1 cup buttermilk

3 tablespoons sour cream

2 tablespoons extra virgin olive oil

2 tablespoons white balsamic vinegar

1 teaspoon Dijon mustard

1 small garlic clove, finely grated

1lb red bitter greens, a mixture of Treviso (the one that looks like purple quills), radicchio and red Belgian endive is ideal

⅔ cup walnuts, lightly toasted

⅓ cup crumbled Cashel Blue cheese

TAMARIND MACKEREL WITH MANGO, LIME & CHILI SALAD

People are divided about mackerel and most don't view it positively, partly because it's strong, very much itself. It's impossible to mute mackerel, but its oiliness is brilliant with chili, rhubarb, ginger, turmeric, tamarind… all the flavors that more subtle ingredients end up fighting with. You can serve the fish with rice, but they're also excellent with bread (mackerel are served stuffed into bread in Istanbul, as street food). Check with your fish market to see if they can get Boston mackerel for you. If they can't, the recipe also works well with salmon fillets. Just spread the tamarind paste over them and bake for 12 minutes at 400°F.

Mix together the garlic, ginger, and all the spices for the mackerel, adding the lime juice, sugar, oil, and seasoning. Spread this all over each fish, inside and out. Cover and put in the refrigerator for about 15 minutes.

Preheat the oven to 400°F.

Now make the salad. Peel the mangoes and cut off the 'cheeks' (the fleshy bits that lie alongside the stone). Cut the cheeks into neat slices. (Use the rest of the flesh from the mangoes for something else… or eat it.)

Put the mango slices in a serving bowl and add the lime juice, chilies, some salt, and the cilantro, and toss.

Line a roasting pan with foil or parchment paper and put the mackerel in it. Roast the mackerel for 20 minutes (if the fish are very big, they might need a little longer; make sure the flesh near the bone is opaque).

Squeeze some lime juice over the fish and serve with rice, or warmed naan bread and yogurt, lime wedges, and the mango and chili salad.

SERVES 4

FOR THE FISH

2 garlic cloves, finely grated

1½in fresh ginger, peeled and finely grated

¾ teaspoon ground turmeric

1½ teaspoons ground cumin

½ teaspoon ground fenugreek

2½ tablespoons tamarind paste

¼ cup lime juice, plus more to serve, plus lime wedges to serve

1 tablespoon light brown sugar

2 tablespoons peanut oil

sea salt flakes and freshly ground black pepper

4 whole Boston mackerel, gutted and washed, or 4 ¼lb salmon fillets

rice, or warmed naan bread and plain yogurt, to serve

FOR THE SALAD

2 just-ripe or slightly under-ripe mangoes

juice of 2 limes

1 red Fresno chlli and 1 green chilli, halved, seeded, and very finely shredded

½ cup cilantro leaves and stalks (make sure the stalks aren't too long or thick)

SLOW-ROAST HOISIN PORK BUTT
WITH RADISH & CUCUMBER SALAD

SERVES 6

FOR THE PORK

4¼lbs boned pork butt

½ cup soy sauce

½ cup clear honey

½ cup hoisin sauce

½ cup amontillado sherry

2 teaspoons five spice powder

1¼in fresh ginger, peeled and finely grated

TO SERVE

boiled rice, or soft white bread rolls

Radish & Cucumber Salad (see overleaf), to serve

crisp lettuce leaves

It's really important to get excellent pork for this. A roast from the supermarket won't be good enough, either in flavor or texture. Go to your butcher. Apart from basting the meat for the last hour of cooking, this is pretty hassle-free.

Remove the skin from the pork—or ask your butcher to do it for you—and discard. Leave the fat on.

Mix together all the other ingredients for the pork in a small bowl to make a marinade. Put this with the pork in a large plastic food storage bag, if possible, or a roasting pan. Marinate in the refrigerator for 24–48 hours, turning the meat over every so often.

Bring the pork to room temperature by removing it from the refrigerator for at least 1 hour before you are going to cook it.

Preheat the oven to 275°F.

Put the pork into a roasting pan in which it will fit snugly (if there is a lot of room around it, the juices and the marinade will just run off and burn) and pour the marinade into a saucepan. Roast the pork for 4½–5 hours, or until the meat is soft and melting. Bring the marinade to a boil, then remove from the heat (it's very important to reheat the marinade to the boiling point, so it's safe for you to use it to baste the partly-cooked pork).

Now ladle some of the marinade over the pork and return to the oven. Keep adding more of the marinade and basting the pork every 10 minutes for the next hour. Turn it over every time you do this. The pork should end up dark and glossy. If the roast starts to get too dark on the outside, cover it with foil.

continued >

FOR THE SALAD

3 tablespoons unseasoned
rice vinegar

3 teaspoons superfine sugar

pinch of fine sea salt

¾in fresh ginger, peeled and
finely grated

1 large garlic clove, very
finely chopped or grated

1 cucumber, chilled

⅔lb radishes (a mixture
of colors if possible),
quartered, or cut into
eighths if they're big

1 teaspoon toasted sesame
oil

1 teaspoon toasted sesame
seeds (a mixture of white
and black, if you like)

To make the salad, mix the vinegar, sugar, salt, ginger, and garlic together. Peel the cucumber in stripes. Halve it along its length and scoop out the seeds, then cut it into 1½in lengths. Bash these with a mallet or a rolling pin. Put the cucumber into a serving bowl with the dressing and place in the refrigerator for 20 minutes. When you're ready to eat, add the radishes and the sesame oil and toss everything together. Scatter the sesame seeds on top.

Serve the pork with boiled rice, or in soft white bread rolls, with the radish and cucumber salad, and with crisp lettuce leaves.

VON DIAZ'S SWEET & SOUR CHICKEN & CHORIZO IN ADOBO

SERVES 6

4lb whole chicken

10 garlic cloves, finely grated

2 tablespoons dried oregano

1 tablespoon sea salt flakes and lots of freshly ground black pepper

4 tablespoons extra virgin olive oil

juice of 2 lemons

3 tablespoons unsalted butter

6 Spanish chorizo cooking sausages

packed ¾ cup light brown sugar

¼ cup red wine vinegar

boiled rice, to serve

As soon as I cooked this, it went straight into my core repertoire of oft-repeated dishes. It's from Coconuts & Collards *by American food writer Von Diaz, a book about combining Puerto Rican food (Von was born there) with the food of the American South, where she grew up. The chicken becomes melting and smoky. I've changed Von's recipe a little—adding more liquid and chorizo—with her approval and adapted it so it can be cooked in the oven rather than on the stovetop; it works either way, though the timings are different.*

Put the chicken into a dish or a large plastic food storage bag. In a bowl, mix the garlic, oregano, salt, pepper, olive oil, and lemon juice, and rub this inside the chicken as well as outside. Cover the dish, or seal the bag, and leave in the refrigerator overnight, or for at least 1 hour. Bring it to room temperature.

Preheat the oven to 400°F.

Scrape the marinade off the outside of the bird (or the oregano and garlic will burn) and heat the butter in a casserole dish big enough for the chicken. Brown the chicken, breast side down first, then on the other sides, being careful not to burn it. Take it out and add the sausages to the pan. Brown them all over, then add the sugar and vinegar. Bring to a boil, stirring to help the sugar dissolve, then reduce the heat to low. Push the sausages to the edges of the pan and put the chicken in the middle, breast side down.

Transfer to the oven and cook for 20 minutes. Reduce the oven temperature to 375°F, cover, and cook for a further 30 minutes. Spoon the juices up over the bird, turn it breast side up, and roast for a final 15 minutes, uncovered. Check for doneness by piercing the bird between the leg and body: the juices that run out should be clear, with no trace of pink.

Slice the sausages and carve the chicken, and give everyone some sausage, some chicken, and plenty of the cooking juices. This really calls for boiled rice on the side.

BAKED SEA BASS WITH RAISINS, PRESERVED LEMONS, GINGER & CILANTRO

SERVES 6–8

FOR THE SPICE PASTE

1½in fresh ginger, peeled and finely grated

2 garlic cloves, finely grated

scant ¼ teaspoon cayenne pepper

juice of ½ small lemon

2 tablespoons extra virgin olive oil

sea salt flakes and freshly ground black pepper

FOR THE STUFFING

9 tablespoons unsalted butter, softened

generous ¼ cup almond flour

½ cup raisins, soaked in boiling water for 15 minutes, then drained and patted dry

2 slices of crystallized ginger, very finely chopped

2 preserved lemons, flesh and rind finely chopped, pips removed

1 garlic clove, finely grated

2 tablespoons chopped cilantro leaves

FOR THE FISH

2 x 2lb sea bass (branzino), gutted, scaled and washed

a little extra virgin olive oil

1 unwaxed lemon, finely sliced, plus lemon wedges to serve

couscous, to serve

This sea bass (branzino) dish was inspired by a salmon dish cooked by the late George Perry-Smith many moons ago in The Hole in the Wall restaurant in Bath. His recipe is stuffed with ginger, almonds, and raisins, wrapped in pastry and served with a herb sauce: sauce messine. It has always seemed very medieval to me, its stuffing Arab-influenced. I still make his dish—and love it—but it takes a bit of work and is very rich. This uses similar flavors and ingredients, with the addition of preserved lemons, but is much simpler. You could also use a whole salmon instead.

Preheat the oven to 425°F. Make the spice paste by mixing everything together in a bowl. Make the stuffing in the same way in a separate bowl, adding plenty of seasoning to both mixtures.

Wash the fish to get rid of any blood (it's bitter) and pat dry with paper towels. Put a double layer of parchment into a roasting pan big enough for the fish. Brush the center—where the fish will lie—with olive oil.

Make diagonal slashes in the fish on each side, cutting down to the bone but not through it. Push the spice paste inside the slits on both sides of each fish. Carefully stuff the butter mixture inside, pushing it up into the heads to get all of it in (you're not going to eat the heads, but you will be able to get the stuffing out of it). Put the fish on to the oiled parchment paper. Lay the lemon slices inside and on top, then drizzle with olive oil and season.

Bake for 20 minutes, then check for doneness: the flesh near the bone in the thickest part of the fish should be opaque. If it needs a little longer, return it to the oven for no more than a couple of minutes, then check again.

Serve with lemon wedges and a bowl of couscous tossed with some chopped pistachios, lemon juice, and finely grated lemon zest.

SLOW-COOKED LEG OF LAMB WITH
SHERRY & AUTUMN VEGETABLES

SERVES 8

8 garlic cloves, plus 1 head of garlic, cloves separated

sea salt flakes and freshly ground black pepper

large pinch of saffron threads (optional)

leaves from 8 thyme sprigs, plus 4 whole thyme sprigs

½ cup extra virgin olive oil

4½lbs leg of lamb

1 large onion, cut into wedges

⅔lb thin bunched carrots, or, if you can only find thick ones, halve or quarter them lengthwise

1lb 2oz waxy potatoes, scrubbed and sliced (no need to peel)

1¾ cups amontillado sherry, plus more if needed

Of course the lamb is supposed to be the star here, but the vegetables are a revelation. They soak up the lamb juices as they cook, becoming really imbued with the flavor both of the lamb and of the sherry. You have all you need in one dish here, but if you want something green, make Olive Oil-roasted Sweet & Sour Leaves with Raisins and Pine Nuts (see page 117).

Preheat the oven to 450°F.

Crush the 8 cloves of garlic in a mortar and pestle with some sea salt flakes (the salt flakes act as an abrasive). Grind in the saffron, if using; it will add its flavor, and of course its gorgeous color, but the dish is just as delicious without. Add the thyme leaves, pepper, and olive oil, to make a loose paste.

Make incisions all over the lamb with a knife and slightly loosen the meat around the bone end, too. Push the garlic and herb paste down into these incisions, into the space around the bone and all over the roast. Put into a large roasting pan or a cast-iron casserole dish; you will need to add all the vegetables later, too, so there has to be room for them as well. Season all over.

Roast for 20 minutes, then remove the pan or casserole from the oven. Reduce the oven temperature to 350°F. Put the onion, carrots, the rest of the garlic cloves, potatoes, and thyme sprigs under and around the lamb. Bring the sherry to just under a boil, then pour it over. Cover tightly with a double layer of foil, or the lid, and return to the oven.

Cook for 2½ hours, turning the lamb over about 3 times and checking on the sherry, too: most of it will be absorbed during cooking, but don't let it get dry. If there are a lot of juices, remove the foil or uncover the pot 45 minutes before the end of cooking time, so they can reduce. The lamb should be cooked to softness —if it isn't, cook it for a little longer—and the vegetables completely tender. Serve the lamb with the vegetables and the sherry juices.

GIGOT OF MONKFISH WITH ROAST LEMON SALSA VERDE

This is an expensive dish, but it's a huge treat; one for your best, most appreciative friends. It's called a gigot because the shape of a monkfish tail is like that of a leg of lamb. I love the lemon in the salsa verde, but there are lots of other sauces in the book that would work with this, too: have a look at the Roast Pepper, Caper and Preserved Lemon Relish (see page 207).

Preheat the oven to 325°F.

Put the lemon slices for the salsa verde onto a sheet pan lined with parchment paper. Cook for 25 minutes. Allow to cool a little, then peel the slices off the parchment, put them in a bowl, and cover with the olive oil. Leave to soak for a few hours if you can: the oil slightly softens the rind and, in turn, the slices flavor the oil.

When you're ready to cook, preheat the oven to 450°F. Put a heavy roasting pan over high heat and add 2 tablespoons of the olive oil. Season the fish and brown it all over—it will take about 5 minutes—then put it into the oven. Roast for 25 minutes; the flesh near the bone should be white, not translucent.

Make the salsa verde by putting all the ingredients, except the oil and lemon slices, in a food processor. Pulse-mix, pouring in the lemon-flavored olive oil as you do so (but not the lemon slices yet). Scrape into a bowl. Chop the roast lemon slices and add them to the mixture, seasoning with a little pepper.

Heat the remaining 3 tablespoons of olive oil in a frying pan and sauté the garlic and rosemary until the garlic is golden. Serve the fish, either in the dish in which it has cooked or on a warmed platter, with the garlic and rosemary oil spooned over the top and the roast lemon salsa verde on the side.

SERVES 6

FOR THE SALSA VERDE

1 unwaxed lemon (not too small), cut into slices ⅛in thick

⅔ cup extra virgin olive oil

10 anchovies, drained of oil

15 basil leaves

15 mint leaves

leaves from a 1oz bunch of flat-leaf parsley

¼ tablespoon Dijon mustard

1 garlic clove, chopped

1 tablespoon capers, rinsed, drained, and patted dry

FOR THE FISH

5 tablespoons extra virgin olive oil

sea salt flakes and freshly ground black pepper

3⅓lbs monkfish tail on the bone, skinned and membrane removed

3 garlic cloves, finely sliced

leaves from 4 rosemary sprigs

MELISSA'S BUTTERFLIED LEG OF LAMB WITH YOGURT & HERB SAUCE

This dish is from my friend (and fellow food writer) Melissa Clark. Melissa is the sort of cook who can have twenty people standing around in her kitchen while she throws dinner together. She's not remotely bothered about serving dishes she's never tried before and is a genuinely laidback cook. It's a joy to watch her (I'm going to cook like her when I grow up).

Toast the cumin and coriander seeds in a dry frying pan over medium heat for about 2 minutes. Let them cool, then put them in a food processor with the onion, lime zest and juice, yogurt, mint and cilantro, garlic, chili, and ginger, salt and pepper. Whizz until you have a paste.

Put the lamb in a dish, or a large plastic food storage bag, with the marinade, making sure the marinade covers the flesh as well as the fatty side. Cover with plastic wrap, or seal the bag, then refrigerate for about 6 hours. Bring the meat to room temperature.

Preheat the oven to 425°F.

Lift the lamb out of the marinade, shaking it off. Spread the meat out in a roasting pan, fatty side up, then roast for 15 minutes.

Reduce the oven temperature to 375°F and cook for another 15 minutes. The lamb will be pink. (If you want it more well done, increase the cooking time by 5 minutes.)

Remove from the oven, cover with foil, insulate with kitchen towels or old towels, and leave to rest for 15 minutes.

To make the sauce, just put all the ingredients into a clean food processor bowl and blend. Taste for seasoning.

Slice the meat and arrange it on a warmed platter, spooning over any juices that have come out of it, and scatter with mint and cilantro leaves and some sea salt flakes. Serve immediately, with lime wedges and the yogurt sauce.

SERVES 8

FOR THE LAMB

1½ tablespoons cumin seeds

2 teaspoons coriander seeds

1 onion, chopped

finely grated zest and juice of 1 lime, plus lime wedges to serve

⅔ cup plain yogurt

leaves from 8 mint sprigs, plus mint leaves to serve

scant 2 cups cilantro leaves and stalks, plus cilantro leaves to serve

6 garlic cloves, chopped

1 red Fresno chili, seeded if you want, chopped

1in fresh ginger, peeled and chopped

½ teaspoon sea salt flakes

½ teaspoon freshly ground black pepper

5lb leg of lamb (pre-boned weight), boned and butterflied by your butcher

FOR THE SAUCE

1 cup Greek yogurt

leaves from 8 mint sprigs

2 cups cilantro leaves

5 tablespoons extra virgin olive oil

2 garlic cloves, chopped

1 scallion, trimmed and chopped

finely grated zest of 1 lime

2 tablespoons lime juice

3 tablespoons mayonnaise

sea salt flakes and freshly ground black pepper

BAKED SEA BASS WITH
ASIAN DRESSING

*This is a gorgeous looking dish and seems much more impressive
than it really is (which is, after all, just roast fish). Serve with
boiled rice and a salad, or with stir-fried bok choy.*

Preheat the oven to 400°F.

Put a double layer of parchment paper into a roasting pan or onto a sheet pan
with a lip. It obviously needs to be big enough to hold the fish.

Put the chili, ginger, garlic, the ¾ cup of cilantro, and the lime zest into a
mortar with some salt and pound them together, adding 1 tablespoon of the
oil, until you have a rough paste. Add the lime juice.

Put the fish on the parchment paper. Make 4 slits in both sides of each fish,
without cutting through the bone, and push the paste into them. Stuff the fish
with the scallions. Rub the rest of the oil over the fish on both sides and season
with salt. Bake for 20 minutes, then check for doneness: the flesh near the
bone at the thickest part should be opaque, not translucent.

Make the dressing by mixing together the lime juice, sugar, fish sauce, and
chili. Serve the fish with the dressing on the side, or spoon it over the top.
Scatter with the ¼ cup cilantro leaves and serve with lime wedges.

SERVES 6

FOR THE FISH
1 red Fresno chili, halved,
seeded, and chopped

1¼in fresh ginger, peeled
and finely grated

3 garlic cloves, finely grated

¾ cup cilantro leaves,
roughly chopped, plus
¼ cup cilantro leaves
to serve

finely grated zest of 2 limes,
plus the juice of ½ lime, plus
lime wedges to serve

sea salt flakes

2 tablespoons peanut oil

2 x 2lb sea bass (branzino),
gutted, scaled and washed

6 scallions, trimmed and
roughly chopped

FOR THE DRESSING
juice of 1 lime

2 tablespoons superfine
sugar

⅓ cup fish sauce

1 red Fresno chili, halved,
seeded, and very thinly sliced

LAMB SHOULDER WITH HONEY, HERBS & LEMON-CAPER RELISH

This really shows what roasting can do. You put a big square of meat—not a prime cut—into the oven and, with a little attention (just make sure there's always some liquid in the roasting pan) and a lot of herbs you end up with a melting mass of delicious meat.

Preheat the oven to 400°F. Put all the herb leaves (not the whole sprigs,) and the dried oregano in a mortar with the salt, pepper, and olive oil and grind everything together. Score the lamb fat—without cutting into the meat—and rub the herb mixture all over it, pushing it down into the slashes. Scatter the herb sprigs and all the garlic cloves in a roasting pan that will hold the lamb snugly. Set the lamb on top; the garlic and the herbs must be underneath, or they will burn. Squeeze the lemon juice over, then pour half the wine into the pan. Cover with a double layer of foil, sealing it tightly around the edges.

Put the pan into the oven and immediately reduce the temperature to 300°F, and cook for 3½–4 hours. Check every so often to see whether you need to add any more wine (just enough to keep the pan moist). The meat is ready when it is falling off the bone. When there are just 30 minutes cooking time left, drizzle the honey on top. Once it's cooked, lay some towels over the foil and leave the lamb to rest for 15 minutes.

To make the relish, remove the lemon zest from 1 lemon with a zester, then roughly chop the zest. Peel the white pith away from the same lemon, then remove all the peel and pith from the other. Remove the flesh from both: using a very sharp knife, cut between each segment and carefully ease it out. Chop the flesh into little pieces and put it in a bowl with the zest, olive oil, honey, vinegar, and lemon juice. Add the capers to the bowl with the garlic. Stir and taste for balance: remember this will be served with fatty lamb that can take a relish that's assertive and quite acidic. Just when you are about to serve, add the mint leaves (they turn black if they sit in acid for too long).

SERVES 6

FOR THE LAMB

2 tbsp lemon thyme leaves, plus another dozen whole sprigs

6 rosemary sprigs, leaves removed and chopped, plus another dozen whole sprigs

1 tablespoon dried oregano

1 tablespoon sea salt flakes

freshly ground black pepper

2 tablespoons extra virgin olive oil

4½lbs lamb shoulder on the bone

1 head of garlic, cloves separated

juice of 1 lemon

1 cup dry white wine

2 tablespoons honey (a floral or herbal type, such as lavender or thyme)

FOR THE RELISH

2 unwaxed lemons

¼ cup extra virgin olive oil

2 tablespoons honey

1 tablespoon white balsamic vinegar

2 tablespoons lemon juice, or to taste

2 tablespoons capers, drained, rinsed, and patted dry

½ small garlic clove, finely grated

leaves from 12 mint sprigs, torn

GARLIC & OREGANO CHICKEN WITH CHIPOTLE ALLIOLI

If you can buy dried Mexican oregano, which is a little different from the European type, then do (you can find it online). The allioli may seem an effort too far—if so, mix some good bought mayonnaise with chipotle paste.

To spatchcock the chicken, set the bird on a work surface, breast side down, legs towards you. Using good kitchen scissors or poultry shears, cut through the flesh and bone along both sides of the backbone. Remove the backbone (you can keep it for stock). Open the chicken, turn it over, then flatten it by pressing hard on the breastbone with the heel of your hand. You'll feel it breaking and flattening under your hand. Remove any big globules of fat and neaten the ragged bits of skin. Now you have a spatchcocked bird.

Put the chicken into a dish that fits in your refrigerator. Mix all the other ingredients to make a marinade. Gently loosen the skin of the breast, pushing your fingers between the skin and flesh. Work your way under the skin down to the legs. Spoon some marinade in here, then spread it over the chicken on both sides. Cover and put into the refrigerator for a few hours if you can, turning it once. Bring the bird to room temperature.

Preheat the oven to 400°F. Put the chicken into a roasting pan and roast for 1 hour, basting a few times during the cooking.

Make the allioli while the chicken is cooking. Mix the egg yolk, mustard, and garlic in a bowl. Using electric beaters or a wooden spoon, gradually add the oils in little drops, making sure each is incorporated before you add the next. If it splits, start again with a new egg yolk and gradually add the curdled mixture. Add the chipotle paste, lemon juice to taste (start with about 1 tablespoon), and seasoning. If you're making this more than 1 hour ahead, cover and keep it in the fridge, stirring it when you take it out. (Don't serve it cold from the refrigerator.)

Check to see if the chicken is cooked properly (*see* page 185). Cut into pieces and serve with the chipotle allioli. Roasted sweet potato wedges are brilliant with it.

SERVES 6

FOR THE CHICKEN

4lb whole chicken

10 garlic cloves, finely grated

½ tablespoon sea salt flakes

1 red Fresno chili, halved, seeded, and finely chopped

1½ tablespoons dried oregano

2 tablespoons extra virgin olive oil

juice of 1 lemon

roast sweet potato wedges, to serve (optional)

FOR THE CHIPOTLE ALLIOLI

1 egg yolk

1 teaspoon Dijon mustard

2 garlic cloves, finely grated

½ cup mixed peanut and extra virgin olive oils

1 tablespoon chipotle paste

lemon juice, to taste

sea salt flakes and freshly ground black pepper

ROAST LAMB WITH APPLES, APPLE BRANDY & CREAM

Very old-fashioned (it's the cream), but very good. A dish to have with cider. I make it with apple brandy but, of course, you can use French Calvados.

SERVES 6

3⅓lbs leg of lamb

6 garlic cloves, cut into fine slivers

leaves from 4 thyme sprigs

2 tablespoons unsalted butter

sea salt flakes and freshly ground black pepper

2 cups dry hard cider

6 small tart apples

¼ cup apple brandy, or Calvados

2 cups low-sodium chicken stock

½ cup heavy cream

2 teaspoons apple jelly (optional)

Preheat the oven to 400°F.

Make small incisions all over the lamb with a very sharp knife, then stuff each slit with a sliver of garlic and a little bit of thyme. Rub the butter all over the lamb, stuffing some of it down inside the incisions. Put in a roasting pan big enough to hold the lamb and—eventually—the apples, too. Season.

Roast for 20 minutes, then reduce the oven temperature to 375°F. Pour a scant 1 cup of the cider around the lamb, then put the apples in, too. Roast for 45 minutes. This will give you very pink lamb. If you prefer it more well done, cook it for a little longer.

Pour the cooking juices into a measuring cup, but be careful with the apples as you do so, because you want them to stay intact. Leave the lamb and the apples to sit and rest, covered and insulated with towels, while you make the sauce.

Add ice cubes to the cooking juices to drive the fat to the surface; skim it off.

Put the apple brandy, cooking juices, and the remaining cider into a saucepan and bring to a boil. Boil until the liquid is reduced by two-thirds, then add the stock. Boil until this, too, is reduced by two-thirds, then add the cream. Boil until slightly syrupy (it doesn't have to be thick, just not as thin as the cooking juices were). If you want the sauce to be a little sweeter, add the apple jelly and allow it to melt into the sauce. Serve the lamb on a warmed platter with the apples around it and the cider sauce in a sauceboat.

POUSSINS WITH BLACK OLIVE & ANCHOVY BUTTER

SERVES 4

2 tablespoons finely chopped pitted black olives (pitted weight)

8 anchovies, drained of oil and chopped

5 tablespoons unsalted butter, softened

1 garlic clove, finely grated

sea salt flakes and freshly ground black pepper

1lb waxy potatoes, such as Yukon Gold, scrubbed

½–1 teaspoon crushed red pepper

leaves from 4 rosemary sprigs

2 tablespoons extra virgin olive oil

4 1lb poussins, or 2 2lb Cornish game hens split into halves

green salad, or roasted vegetables, to serve

Ever since I read about Alice Waters serving black olive and anchovy butter at Chez Panisse, I have been making it myself. This couldn't be simpler, but the end result delivers much more than you expect...though you can't go wrong with chicken and melting butter, salty with anchovies and inky with olives. If you can't find poussins, you can replace them with Cornish game hens split in half (see page 166). Serve with watercress or roast red peppers and baby potatoes cooked with rosemary (see page 107).

Preheat the oven to 375°F.

Put the olives, anchovies, butter, garlic, and black pepper into a mortar and pestle and either pound or mash. (You can also do this with a fork and bowl, although the ingredients don't end up as well incorporated.)

Cut the potatoes into chunks—roughly ¾in square—and put them into a roasting pan in which they can lie in a single layer, with room for the poussins on top. Add the crushed red pepper, rosemary leaves, seasoning, and about two-thirds of the olive oil and toss all this with the potatoes.

Gently lift the skin on the breast of the poussins—be careful not to tear it—and push the butter down under the skin of each bird (if you can get as far as the legs, pushing some in there too, so much the better, but it's hard to do this without ripping the skin). Don't use all the butter, keep some for melting on the poussins once they're cooked.

Put the poussins on top of the potatoes, brush the remaining oil on the birds, and season. Roast for 50 minutes (or 35-40 minutes if you're using Cornish game hen halves). Transfer the poussins and the potatoes to a warmed platter and put some of the remaining butter to melt on top of the poussins. Serve immediately.

This is lovely with a green salad, but some kind of roasted vegetable is good too (eggplant, fennel, tomatoes, or peppers, depending on the time of year).

BAKED ANCHOVY-STUFFED RED MULLET WITH FENNEL

They are such wonderful little fish, red mullet, both because of their color and small tender flakes, and because they arrive in winter looking as if they've come straight from a blue-sky summer. If you can't find red mullet, use ocean perch or Pacific rockfish instead. There's quite a lot of stuffing here—more than will, strictly, fit inside the fish—but let it spill out into the dish. The fish aren't in the oven for long, so the stuffing doesn't get dry, it just soaks up the juices.

Preheat the oven to 375°F.

Remove any fronds from the fennel and reserve. Trim the tips—they are coarse—quarter the bulb(s), and trim the bottom of each piece. Slice the fennel lengthwise into thin wedges, about ¼in at the thickest part. Toss the fennel into a roasting pan or a 12in shallow casserole with the onion, salt and pepper, a couple of tablespoons of olive oil, and the lemon juice. Bake in the oven for 15 minutes.

Mix all the ingredients for the stuffing with some seasoning and add a little olive oil (the mixture should be moist, but not sloppy). Season the cavities of the fish, then stuff them with the anchovy mixture, pushing it up into the head so you can get plenty inside each one.

Put the fish on top of the vegetables, season, then drizzle with a little olive oil. Scatter on the fennel fronds.

Bake for 20 minutes. The flesh should be opaque near the bone at the thickest part—not at all translucent—and the vegetables tender. Serve with lemon wedges and good bread.

SERVES 4

FOR THE FISH AND FENNEL

1 large or 2 medium fennel bulbs

1 red onion, sliced into fine wedges no more than ¼in at the thick end

sea salt flakes and freshly ground black pepper

extra virgin olive oil

juice of 1 lemon, plus lemon wedges to serve

4 medium whole red mullet, Pacific rockfish, or ocean perch, about ¾lb each, gutted, scaled, and washed

good bread, to serve

FOR THE STUFFING

10 anchovies, drained of oil and finely chopped

⅔ cup fresh white breadcrumbs

2 garlic cloves, finely grated

1 plum tomato, finely chopped

1 tablespoon finely chopped flat-leaf parsley leaves

ENDLESS EMBELLISHMENTS

Roasted foods—whole chickens or legs of lamb, fish, root vegetables or softer Mediterranean vegetables—are basic; it isn't difficult to cook them. But their character can be completely changed depending on what you serve with them. These salsas and relishes—accessories, if you like—bring their own personality and can be made while your chicken thighs or peppers are being transformed by the heat of the oven. Most of them require only chopping and mixing. Each serves 4–6.

ANCHOVY, OLIVE, & CAPER DRESSING

Gently heat ½ cup of extra virgin olive oil and add 2 finely sliced garlic cloves. Cook for 1 minute, then add 12 drained, chopped anchovies. Cook gently, pressing with the back of a spoon until they "melt." Add about a dozen chopped pitted black olives, a good pinch of crushed red pepper, 1½ tablespoons of soaked, drained, and patted dry capers, 1½ tablespoons of lemon juice, and 2 tablespoons of finely chopped flat-leaf parsley leaves. Good with steak or roast beef or lamb, roast tomatoes or peppers, or roast fish.

ARTICHOKE & BASIL MAYO

This is based on a recipe from the American chef and vegetable maestro Joshua McFadden. It's wonderful with roasted Mediterranean vegetables, especially tomatoes, slices of eggplant, and peppers; try it with those in ciabatta sandwiches. It's also lovely with roast chicken and lamb: have it on the side with basic chicken thighs roasted with potatoes and onions, or lamb loin (*see* page 22), or roast sea bass or bream. Put 6 drained jarred artichoke hearts into a blender with a generous handful of basil leaves and pulse a few times. Add scant 1 cup of mayonnaise and 1 egg yolk. Whizz, then add 1 tablespoon of lemon juice. With the motor running, gradually add ¼ cup of extra virgin olive oil. Taste for seasoning and balance: you might want a little more lemon juice.

YOGURT & PRESERVED LEMON DRESSING

Chop the flesh and rind of 2 preserved lemons—discard any seeds—and stir it into ⅔ cup of Greek yogurt along with 2 tablespoons of brine from the preserved lemon jar and 1 garlic clove, finely grated. Serve with roast tomatoes, eggplants, peppers, or pumpkin.

ARTICHOKE & GREEN OLIVE TAPENADE

Purée scant 1 cup of drained jarred artichoke hearts, 3 tablespoons of pitted green olives, 3 tablespoons of blanched almonds, 1 garlic clove, chopped, a pinch of crushed red pepper, the juice of ½ lemon, and 5 tablespoons of extra virgin olive oil with salt and pepper. Particularly good with fish, chicken, roast tomatoes, and peppers.

AVOCADO, CILANTRO, & PICKLED CHILI RELISH

Chop the flesh of 2 just-ripe avocados and put it in a bowl with the juice of 1 lime, ½lb of well-flavored tomatoes, finely chopped, 2 scallions, also finely chopped, 1 teaspoon of ground cumin, 1 red Fresno chili, seeded and finely chopped, 3 tablespoons of finely chopped cilantro leaves, 2 pickled chilies, chopped, 1 garlic clove, finely grated, 5 tablespoons of extra virgin olive oil, salt, and pepper. Taste: you may need more lime juice. Serve with baked potatoes (regular or sweet) along with sour cream, baked fish of any type, or roast chicken or pork.

GEORGIAN ADJIKA

Put 4 garlic cloves and 1 celery stalk, both roughly chopped, into a food processor with 4 red Fresno chilies and 1 red pepper, both chopped and seeded. Pulse-blend to a salsa-like mixture. Add 2 cups each of dill and cilantro leaves and pulse-blend again. Scrape into a bowl and add seasoning, 3½ tablespoons of red wine vinegar, and ¼ cup of extra virgin olive oil. Good with chicken and lamb. It is hot, so be careful. I serve it with yogurt (in case you need to put the fire out).

THAI NAM JIM DRESSING

Put 2 garlic cloves, chopped, into a mortar with a pinch of sea salt flakes—the salt acts as an abrasive—and ⅔ cup roughly chopped cilantro leaves, and pound to a rough paste. Add 1 red Fresno chili, chopped (leave the seeds in) and 2 tablespoons of palm sugar or light brown sugar, and pound some more. Stir in 2 tablespoons of fish sauce, 2½ tablespoons of lime juice, and 2 small shallots, very thinly chopped. Good with baked fish and roast chicken or pork.

ROAST PEPPER, CAPER, & PRESERVED LEMON RELISH

In a bowl, stir together ½ roasted red bell pepper, chopped, 2 tablespoons of white balsamic vinegar, ⅓ cup of extra virgin olive oil, the rind of 1 preserved lemon, finely chopped, 1 tablespoon of rinsed, drained, and patted dry capers, 1 red Fresno chili, seeded and finely chopped, and 3 tablespoons of chopped cilantro leaves (mint is good as well). Lovely with roast fish or lamb: try it with lamb loin fillets (*see* page 22), cooked without the peas.

SMOKY CHIMICHURRI

A riff on a classic sauce used in Argentina and Uruguay and perfect with beef, though it's also good on potatoes and roast tomatoes. Put 4 garlic cloves, chopped, into a food processor with 4 cups of flat-leaf parsley leaves and 5 cups of cilantro leaves, and add 5 tablespoons of extra virgin olive oil (a buttery one). Pour in 5 tablespoons of cider vinegar and ¼ teaspoon of smoked paprika. Pulse-blend, then stir in 1 green chili, seeded and finely chopped, 4 trimmed and chopped scallions, and salt and pepper.

HOT SOUR-SWEET ASIAN SAUCE

This—which is quite like Vietnamese *nuoc cham*, but not the same—is intensely salty, sour, and sweet and can sit in the refrigerator for about 5 days. It's worth making in quantity, though you can also halve it. Mix 5 tablespoons of boiling water (less if you want the sauce to be more intense) with ¼ cup of superfine sugar or palm sugar. Stir well to dissolve the sugar. Add 6–8 red chilies, halved, deseeded, and chopped, ½ cup of fish sauce, 5 tablespoons of unseasoned rice vinegar, the juice of 1–2 limes, 4 garlic cloves, finely grated, and ¾in of fresh ginger, peeled, and finely grated. Great with roast chicken and fish, though I find it totally addictive and would put it on nearly anything.

MANGO & TAMARIND RELISH

Peel 2 under-ripe mangoes and remove the flesh as neatly as possible. Cut it into small cubes and put in a saucepan with 1 red and 1 green chili, both halved, seeded, and finely chopped. Add 2 tablespoons of tamarind paste, 1 tablespoon of light brown sugar, and ¼ cup of water. Set over medium heat and cook for 4 minutes, stirring from time to time (you can serve this raw, but I like it a little cooked). Remove from the heat and add the juice of 1 lime. Just before serving, stir in 2 tablespoons of chopped cilantro leaves. Good with roast chicken, pork, or baked fish, such as mackerel, salmon, or sea bass (branzino). This takes on an Indian accent if you add a little ground cumin, turmeric, and ginger.

PARSLEY, TOMATO, & POMEGRANATE RELISH

Halve and seed ¼lb of tomatoes and finely chop the flesh. Mix in the finely chopped leaves from 4oz of flat-leaf parsley, ½ small red onion, finely chopped, 1 small garlic clove, finely grated, 1 tablespoon of lemon juice, ¼ cup of extra virgin olive oil, 1 tablespoon of pomegranate molasses, the seeds from ½ pomegranate, and seasoning. Serve with fish, chicken, lamb, or roast Mediterranean vegetables.

POT-ROAST INDIAN-SPICED CHICKEN WITH COCONUT

This dish is not from India. I just made it up to feed my longing for Indian spices. It's slightly sweet—because of the sweet potatoes —and rich with ginger and coconut.

Preheat the oven to 400°F.

Start by making the spice paste. Put the mustard seeds in a frying pan over medium heat and cook until the seeds start to pop (this happens in less than a minute). Add the peppercorns, cumin and coriander seeds, garam masala, turmeric, and cinnamon. Cook for 2 minutes.

Scrape the spice mix into a mini food processor with the chilies, garlic, ginger, malt vinegar, and oil. Process to a paste. If you don't have a mini food processor, put the dry spices into a mortar, add the chilies, garlic, and ginger, and grind to a paste, gradually adding the vinegar and oil. Rub about half the spice paste all over the chicken and season the bird in the cavity and outside.

Heat the oil in a casserole dish big enough to hold the chicken. Sauté the onion until soft and golden, then add the garlic, ginger, and the rest of the spice paste and cook for 2 minutes. Add the tomatoes, seasoning, and sugar, if using, and cook for another 4 minutes or so, or until it has reduced a little and isn't quite as sloppy. Add the coconut cream and bring to just under a boil, then put the chicken in with the sweet potatoes, spoon over the juices, and put into the oven, uncovered.

Cook for 20 minutes, then cover, reduce the oven temperature to 375°F, and cook for a further 30 minutes. Spoon the juices over the bird and return it to the oven for a final 15 minutes, uncovered. Check for doneness by piercing the chicken between the leg and the main body: the juices that run out should be clear, with no trace of pink.

Scatter the cilantro over everything and serve the chicken from the pot. You'll need boiled rice or naan bread on the side, and maybe some raita.

SERVES 6

FOR THE SPICE PASTE

1 teaspoon black mustard seeds

1 teaspoon black peppercorns

1 tablespoon cumin seeds

1 tablespoon coriander seeds

1 teaspoon garam masala

½ teaspoon ground turmeric

¼ teaspoon ground cinnamon

2 red Fresno chilies, halved and seeded

3 garlic cloves, finely grated

¾in fresh ginger, peeled and chopped

2 tablespoons malt vinegar

1 tablespoon peanut oil

FOR THE CHICKEN

4lb whole chicken

sea salt flakes and freshly ground black pepper

1 tablespoon peanut oil

1 large onion, finely chopped

3 garlic cloves, finely grated

¾in fresh ginger, peeled and finely grated

14oz can of cherry tomatoes in thick juice

1 teaspoon light brown sugar (optional)

14oz can of coconut cream

1lb sweet potatoes, scrubbed, cut into chunks (peel them if you want to)

½ cup roughly chopped cilantro leaves

boiled rice, naan bread and raita (optional), to serve

SOMETHING SWEET

DESSERTS & CAKE

CHOCOLATE & RED WINE CAKE

*OK, not exactly throw-it-in-the-oven, but nevertheless an easy
cake that can be served for afternoon tea as well as for dessert.
The orange-red wine balance is delicate, so don't add any more
zest than suggested or the flavor of the wine will disappear.
Astonishingly, despite all that chocolate, you can taste it.*

Preheat the oven to 350°F. Butter a 9in springform cake pan and line the
bottom with parchment paper.

Put the chocolate in a heatproof bowl set over a pan of gently simmering
water (the bottom of the bowl shouldn't touch the water). Melt the chocolate,
stirring a little to help it along. Remove the bowl and leave it to cool a little.

Cream the butter and sugar with electric beaters until lighter in color and
fluffy. Gradually add the eggs, beating well after each addition.

In a bowl, sift together the cocoa, flour, baking powder, and salt, then fold
the mixture into the batter. Stir in the red wine and the orange zest, then the
melted chocolate. Scrape into the prepared pan and bake for 40 minutes, or
until a skewer inserted into the middle comes out clean. Allow the cake to cool
in the pan, then turn it out onto a wire rack to cool completely.

For the glaze, put the chocolate into a heatproof bowl and melt as before.
Stir in the cream with the port until the mixture is smooth, then whisk in the
confectioners' sugar. Leave this to cool a little (though don't leave it until it
has set), then pour it over the cake. Let the glaze set a bit before serving.

A glass of red dessert wine (look for Maury from France, or the Greek sweet
red wine Mavrodaphne) is lovely with this.

SERVES 10

FOR THE CAKE

1¾ sticks (7oz) unsalted
butter, at room temperature,
plus more for the pan

5½oz 70% cocoa solids
dark chocolate, broken
into pieces

1½ cups dark
brown sugar

4 extra-large eggs, at room
temperature, lightly beaten

3 tablespoons cocoa powder

1¾ cups all-purpose flour

1 teaspoon baking powder

pinch of fine sea salt

½ cup full-bodied red wine
(Merlot is perfect here)

finely grated zest of
1 orange

FOR THE GLAZE

4½oz 70% cocoa solids
dark chocolate, broken
into pieces

½ cup heavy cream

2 tablespoons port

3 tablespoons confectioners'
sugar, sifted

BAKED RICE PUDDING WITH
QUINCE JELLY & BLACKBERRIES

It took me years to get baked rice pudding right (I kept trying to cook it too quickly). The nutmeggy skin and swollen creamy grains are the gorgeous result of slow baking in the oven. If you have blackcurrant jelly, or other sweet homemade jellies, use those instead of quince jelly.

Preheat the oven to 325°F and butter a 2-quart baking dish.

Put the butter, sugar, rice, milk, and cream into a saucepan and bring gently to a boil, stirring to help the sugar dissolve. Add the salt, nutmeg, lemon zest, and vanilla extract and return to a simmer.

Simmer for about 4 minutes, stirring all the time, until you can feel that the rice grains have become slightly (only slightly) swollen. Pour the mixture into the prepared dish and bake for 2 hours. By this time the rice should be creamy and cooked, but shouldn't be dry or overly sticky.

As the pudding looks beautiful baked—it develops a lovely golden skin on top—take it to the table in the baking dish, and put the quince jelly and the blackberries in separate serving bowls so people can help themselves.

SERVES 4–6

FOR THE RICE PUDDING

3½ tablespoons unsalted butter, plus more for the dish

3 tablespoons superfine sugar

scant ½ cup short-grain rice (not risotto rice)

1 quart whole milk

⅔ cup heavy cream

pinch of salt

lots of freshly grated nutmeg

finely grated zest of ½ unwaxed lemon

¼ teaspoon vanilla extract

TO SERVE

quince jelly (blackcurrant jelly is a good substitute)

⅓lb blackberries

GINGER-ROASTED PLUMS WITH LIME, RUM & BROWN SUGAR CREAM

This is best made with plums that have a strong flavor and will hold their shape: crimson tart-sweet fruits. You need to judge for doneness, as the cooking time depends on how ripe your plums are (they can take as long as 30 minutes if they're hard), but roasting does transform the most unpromising and under-ripe specimens. You can also make this dish with apricots, but they take a bit less cooking time.

Make the cream about 12 hours before you want to serve it. Lightly whip the heavy cream, then fold in the yogurt. Put this in a bowl and sprinkle evenly with the sugar. Cover with plastic wrap and refrigerate. The sugar will become soft and molasses-like.

Preheat the oven to 375°F.

Put the plums into a roasting pan or a big ovenproof dish or gratin dish in which they can lie in a single layer (snugly; you don't want the juices around them to reduce and burn). Arrange the fruits so they are cut sides up. Scatter the crystallized ginger around the plums. Mix the sugar with the ground ginger and sprinkle it over the top. Squeeze the lime juice over and tuck the pieces of lime zest under the fruits, then pour the ⅔ cup rum around them.

Bake for 15–30 minutes (how long it takes depends on the ripeness of the plums). The fruit should be tender when pierced with a sharp knife, but not collapsing. Leave to cool completely; the juices should thicken as they cool. If they aren't thick enough, drain off the juices and boil them in a saucepan until they become more syrupy. Add the remaining 3 tablespoons of rum. Serve the plums, at room temperature, with the brown sugar cream.

SERVES 6

FOR THE CREAM

¾ cup plus 2 tablespoons heavy cream

⅔ cup Greek yogurt

3–4 heaping tablespoons dark brown sugar

FOR THE PLUMS

1¾lbs plums (preferably crimson-fleshed), halved and pitted

2 slices of crystallized ginger, very finely chopped

½ cup light brown sugar

½ teaspoon ground ginger

3 broad strips of lime zest, plus juice of 1 lime

⅔ cup dark rum, plus 3 tablespoons

ROASTED STONE FRUIT WITH ALMOND & ORANGE FLOWER CRUMBS

SERVES 8

2lb stone fruit: a mixture of peaches, nectarines, plums, and apricots is good here

2 tablespoons superfine sugar

finely grated zest of 1 unwaxed lemon, plus juice of ½ lemon

2½oz good-quality marzipan

½ tablespoon orange flower water

⅓ cup all-purpose flour

¼ cup almond flour

4 tablespoons cold unsalted butter, cut into cubes

2 tablespoons sliced almonds

confectioners' sugar, to dust (optional)

whipped cream or crème fraîche, to serve

I like crumble—who doesn't?—but it can be a bit stodgy, more about the crumble than the fruit. In this dish, the fruit shines more—it gets gorgeous caramelized edges—and the "crumble" is rich with nuggets of marzipan and scented with orange flower water. This is a big dessert and I usually have leftovers, but that means I can eat them for breakfast.

Preheat the oven to 400°F.

Halve and pit all the fruit. Cut the larger fruits—peaches and nectarines—into 6 wedges (each half into 3). Put all the fruit into a dish, sprinkle it with the sugar, lemon zest, and lemon juice, and turn it over with your hands. Take 1oz of the marzipan and put little nuggets of this in among the fruit. Break the rest of the marzipan into little balls, but reserve it for now. Sprinkle the orange flower water over the fruit.

Put the flour, almond flour, and butter into a bowl and rub them together with your fingertips. You want to end up with a mixture that looks like small pebbles and gravel. Sprinkle this over the top of the fruit, then put the balls of marzipan on top, too, leaving patches of the fruit completely uncovered. Bake for 30 minutes, or until the fruit is completely tender and the crumbs are golden, scattering over the sliced almonds halfway through the cooking time.

Leave to cool a bit (I like it at room temperature, but you might prefer it warm) and dust a little confectioners' sugar over the top, if you want.

Serve with whipped cream or crème fraîche.

RHUBARB WITH SLOE GIN, ORANGE, & ROSEMARY

SERVES 4

1½lbs hothouse or main crop rhubarb stalks, all about the same thickness

½ cup granulated sugar

finely grated zest of ½ orange

7 tablespoons sloe gin

3 tablespoons orange juice

2 rosemary sprigs, bruised

whipped cream or heavy cream, to serve

I usually bake rhubarb in the oven, rather than poaching it. This way, the pieces stay intact, although you still have to be sure that they don't overcook and collapse, so keep an eye on the dish. Cinnamon, ginger, or star anise work well too, instead of rosemary. If you can't find sloe gin then port is a good substitute.

Preheat the oven to 350°F.

Remove any leaves from the rhubarb and trim the bottoms. Cut into 1¼in lengths and put them into a large ovenproof dish. Scatter the sugar and zest on top and turn it all over with your hands, then pour in the sloe gin, orange juice, and 2 tablespoons of water, and finally tuck the rosemary sprigs under the rhubarb.

Cover tightly with foil, then bake for 30 minutes or so (the time this takes will depend on the thickness of the stalks, start checking after 20 minutes by piercing them with a sharp knife). The rhubarb should be tender, but holding its shape and not collapsing.

Remove from the oven and leave to cool a bit in the dish. Eat warm, at room temperature, or chilled, with whipped cream or heavy cream.

APRICOT & ALMOND CROÛTES

This is really a cheat's Bostock, the French creation where brioche is topped with jam and almond paste (and sometimes fruit) and baked. It is definitely more than just fruit on toast, but it's as simple as that. You need ripe apricots. Unripe fruits won't soften in the time they're in the oven, so, if you can't find good apricots, plums would be better and are just as lovely. And get good brioche; some supermarket brands are a bit dry.

Preheat the oven to 400°F.

Put the brioche slices on a sheet pan or in a roasting pan in which they can lie in a single layer.

Spoon the 2 tablespoons sugar into a small heatproof bowl and pour in ¼ cup of boiling water. Stir until dissolved, then leave this simple syrup to cool. Stir in the amaretto or Marsala.

Spoon the cooled syrup over the brioche slices, covering both sides.

Carefully, because the brioche will be very soft now, butter each slice on both sides.

Arrange chunks of marzipan on top, then add the apricot quarters. Squeeze on the lemon juice and sprinkle with the 4 teaspoons of superfine sugar.

Bake for 25 minutes, sprinkling on the almonds, if using, after 15 minutes. The apricots should be tender and the bread and marzipan both golden.

Leave to cool a little (the slices will be very hot), then sift over some confectioners' sugar, if you want. Serve with crème fraîche.

SERVES 6

6 thick slices of brioche

2 tablespoons superfine sugar, plus 4 teaspoons

¼ cup amaretto or Marsala

5 tablespoons very soft unsalted butter

3¾oz good-quality marzipan, broken into small chunks

12 small ripe apricots, or 6 plums, pitted and quartered

juice of ½ lemon

generous ¼ cup sliced almonds (optional)

confectioners' sugar, to dust (optional)

crème fraîche, to serve

SOUR CHERRY, ROSE & CARDAMOM BRIOCHE PUDDING

I apologize. I nearly always include a recipe for bread pudding in my books, because I keep making new versions and am always in love with the latest incarnation. Get good, fat dried sour cherries for this (and make it with fresh sour cherries when in season). The combination of cardamom and rose water is heaven, but don't overdo the spice. It should feel as if cardamom has "walked through" a dish, leaving its perfume behind; it should never dominate.

SERVES 8

1 cup dried sour cherries

scant ½ cup unsweetened pomegranate juice

1¼ cups heavy cream

1¼ cups whole milk

pinch of sea salt

seeds from 2 cardamom pods, ground

3 extra-large eggs, plus 1 extra-large egg yolk

generous ½ cup superfine sugar

9oz brioche loaf

2½ tablespoons unsalted butter, softened

1 teaspoon rose water, or to taste

squeeze of lemon or lime juice

confectioners' sugar, to dust

Put the dried cherries in a small saucepan and add enough pomegranate juice to just cover. Bring to a boil, then take off the heat and leave the cherries to sit and plump up (they need at least 30 minutes, but longer is fine).

Bring the cream, milk, and salt to a boil in a heavy-bottomed saucepan with the cardamom, then leave for 15 minutes off the heat. Beat the eggs, egg yolk, and sugar together. Pour the warm milk mixture onto this, stirring constantly.

Slice the brioche, butter it, and layer it in a 2 quart ovenproof dish, scattering the soaked cherries and any leftover pomegranate juice on as you layer the bread (try to get most of the cherries under the bread, or they might burn). Add some rose water to the egg and cream mixture—not too much—and a squeeze of lemon or lime juice, then taste it. You should be able to detect the rose water, but it shouldn't be too strong. Brands differ in strength, so you have to taste and decide if you need a little more.

Pour the egg and milk mixture evenly over the layers of bread. Leave the pudding to sit for 30 minutes; this will make it lighter.

Preheat the oven to 375°F.

Put the dish into a roasting pan and carefully pour enough boiling water into the pan to come about one-third of the way up the sides of the dish. Bake for 40–45 minutes, or until puffy, golden, and just set on the top. Remove the dish from the roasting tin and leave to cool slightly—the pudding will continue to cook in the residual heat for a while—then dust with confectioners' sugar before serving.

SERVES 6

6 just-ripe pears

½ cup cassis

1¼ cups red wine

¼ cup superfine sugar

3 bay leaves

5½oz blackberries

CASSIS & BAY-BAKED PEARS
WITH BLACKBERRIES

*Pears are the most adaptable, well-behaved, rewarding fruits
for autumn and winter desserts. Their flesh really sucks up
other flavors, becoming imbued with red wine, Marsala,
cinnamon, star anise, or whatever else you choose. This is
a 'very-beginning-of-autumn' dessert, to be made while
blackberries are still around. Bay is underrated in sweet dishes;
its peppery, slightly menthol flavor is subtle, but it provides a
savory hum. This is best made the day before serving, then the
pears have time to take on the rich color of the wine and cassis.*

Preheat the oven to 375°F.

Halve the pears—you don't need to peel or core them—and put them, cut sides
up, into a gratin dish in which the fruit can sit quite snugly in a single layer.
Pour the cassis and red wine over the pears, sprinkle with the sugar, and tuck
the bay leaves under the fruit.

Bake—spooning the juices over the pears from time to time—until the fruits
are tender right through to the center (how long this takes depends on the
ripeness of the fruit; start checking after 20 minutes, but it could take as long
as 35 minutes). It's a good idea to turn the pears over a couple of times while
they're cooking.

By the time the fruit is cooked, the juice around it won't be thick, but should
be syrupy and sweet enough to serve as it is. If you don't think it is, then
remove the pears and bay leaves and reduce the juices by boiling them for a
little while, leave to cool, then pour them back into the dish with the pears.

Add the berries about 30 minutes before you want to serve, spooning the juices
over them, otherwise they get very soft sitting in the red wine syrup.

BAKED LIME, PASSION FRUIT
& COCONUT PUDDING

SERVES 4–6

9 tablespoons unsalted butter, at room temperature, plus more for the dish

1²⁄₃ cups superfine sugar

4 extra-large eggs, separated

½ cup all-purpose flour

¾ teaspoon baking powder

⅛ teaspoon salt

½ cup dried shredded coconut

1¾ cups whole milk

finely grated zest and juice of 3 limes

5 large, juicy passion fruits, or 6 smaller fruits

confectioners' sugar, to serve

whipped cream, to serve

A riff on the enduring and much-loved Australian classic, lemon delicious pudding. It's miraculous—a citrussy curd-cum-custard forms below the sponge as it cooks—and one of the simplest sweets you can have up your sleeve. A perfect Sunday lunch dessert.

Preheat the oven to 350°F. Butter a 2-quart ovenproof dish.

Throw the butter and sugar into a food processor and process until light and fluffy. Add the egg yolks and whizz the mixture, then add the flour, baking powder, salt, and coconut, alternating with the milk, blending just until you have a smooth batter. Add the lime zest and juice, then scrape the batter into a large bowl.

Halve the passion fruits and scoop the pulp and seeds into a sieve placed over the bowl of batter. Push the pulp through the sieve into the batter, then add two-thirds of the black seeds, too (discard the remaining seeds).

Beat the egg whites until stiff. Using a large metal spoon, fold one-third of them into the batter to lighten it, then fold in the rest. Spoon into the prepared dish and set it in a roasting pan. Pour enough boiling water into the roasting pan to come halfway up the sides of the baking dish and bake for 45 minutes.

Allow the pudding to cool a little when it comes out of the oven, then sift confectioners' sugar over the top and serve with lightly whipped cream.

BAKED NECTARINES WITH PISTACHIOS & ROSE WATER

SERVES 6

6 nectarines, halved and pitted

⅔ cup shelled unsalted pistachios

finely grated zest of ½ unwaxed lemon

1½ tablespoons superfine sugar

1 medium egg, lightly beaten

3 teaspoons rose water

1¼ cups apple juice

confectioners' sugar, to dust

nougat, to serve (optional)

heavy cream, to serve

I prefer nectarines to the more usual peaches for this kind of dish, as their slight tartness contrasts well with the sweet filling. If you don't like rose water, you can use orange flower water instead; I know they're both flower waters, but they give very different results. Serve the nectarines with little pieces of nougat, if you have some.

Preheat the oven to 375°F.

Put the nectarine halves in a gratin dish in which they can lie in a single layer without too much space around them (otherwise the apple juice will reduce and burn).

Crush the pistachios roughly using a mortar and pestle, then mix in the lemon zest, sugar, egg, and 1 teaspoon of the rose water. Fill the cavity of each nectarine with this stuffing, mounding it over the top if you have too much.

Mix the apple juice with the rest of the rose water and pour it around the nectarines. Bake for 30–45 minutes (the time it takes depends on the ripeness of the fruit). The nectarines should be tender and slightly caramelized on top.

Serve the fruit at room temperature, with a little confectioners' sugar sifted on top and some of the cooking juices spooned around, and pieces of nougat, if you like. Cream never goes amiss, of course.

BAKED APPLES WITH TOASTED RYE, MINCEMEAT & APPLE BRANDY CREAM

This recipe came about because I had to use up some mincemeat after Christmas; now I keep mincemeat just so I can make it. If you can't find mincemeat in the grocery store, you can buy it online. Don't use apples that are too small, or you won't have room for the stuffing. The breadcrumbs really do make this.

Preheat the oven to 375°F.

For the rye crumbs, melt the butter in a frying pan, then cook until it starts to brown a little. Remove from the heat and stir in the breadcrumbs and sugar. Spread this out on a baking sheet (it's important that the mixture is not in clumps) and bake for 20 minutes, tossing a few times during baking, until toasted. Let cool.

Slice the top off each apple to make a lid about 2in across, then core each one. Remove a little of the flesh around the core, too (don't throw it away—use it for a smoothie or something).

Put the apples in an ovenproof dish or roasting pan in which they can sit close to each other; you don't want masses of space around them.

Mix the mincemeat with the cranberries, orange zest, and nuts. Spoon this into each apple, sprinkling any leftovers into the dish, then put the apple lids on. Pour the cider around the apples.

Bake for 30–40 minutes, or until the apples are completely tender, spooning the juices up over them every so often. Do keep an eye on the apples, as they can go from tender to burst and falling apart very suddenly.

Whip the cream until it's holding its shape, then whisk in the brown sugar and apple brandy or Calvados. Serve the apples with their juices, adding a dollop of the apple brandy cream and a scattering of the rye crumbs.

SERVES 8

FOR THE APPLES AND TOASTED RYE

1 tablespoon unsalted butter

1 cup coarse rye or pumpernickel breadcrumbs

packed ¼ cup light brown sugar

8 tart apples

8oz mincemeat (I like Robertson's)

½ cup dried cranberries

finely grated zest of ½ orange

2 tablespoons roughly chopped walnuts or hazelnuts

1⅔ cups dry hard cider, plus more if needed

FOR THE CREAM

1¼ cups heavy cream

2½ tablespoons light brown sugar, or to taste

3 tablespoons apple brandy or Calvados

MAIL-ORDER SOURCES

Nearly every ingredient can be bought online nowadays, though I've tried, throughout this book, to suggest alternatives for harder-to-find foods. I don't imagine there is a single food you can't find from the companies below, or if all else fails, Amazon. You probably have your own local butcher or favorite fish market, but I've listed some great online butchers (my own favorite butcher is two bus rides away so I often shop online for meat). We all depend on supermarkets, but even the best are not good for pork—I'd definitely buy that at a good butcher. When buying dry goods, it's best to make a long list of ingredients and get them from one source, as that way you save on delivery costs.

D'ARTAGNAN FOODS

www.dartagnan.com

An excellent online butcher, particularly good for more unusual cuts of meat like poussins.

BELCAMPO

www.belcampo.com

California-based butcher with a completely transparent and sustainable supply chain. Especially good for lamb and pork.

CITARELLA

www.citarella.com

Has every single kind of fish you can think of, including more obscure ones like red mullet.

OAKTOWN SPICE SHOP

www.oaktownspiceshop.com

A fantastic selection of spices from around the world, in a range of package sizes. They also stock single-origin spices with a more transparent supply chain. Check out their spice blends and dried chiles, too.

LA TIENDA

www.tienda.com

Your one-stop shop for all things Spanish. A great place to buy smoked paprika, meats like cooking chorizo, and paella rice. You can also find a range of paella pans here.

99 RANCH

www.99ranch.com

Nationwide pan-Asian grocery store chain that also sells groceries online.

H-MART

www.hmart.com

The online presence of the Korean grocery store chain, and a great place to find ingredients such as gochujang and gochugaru.

KALUSTYAN'S

www.foodsofnations.com

New York-based grocery store that ships nationwide and stocks every single Middle Eastern ingredient you could ever need. Preserved lemons, rosewater, dried lentils, sumac—they're all here.

An Hachette UK Company
www.hachette.co.uk

First published in Great Britain in 2019 by Mitchell Beazley,
a division of Octopus Publishing Group Ltd
Carmelite House
50 Victoria Embankment
London EC4Y 0DZ
www.octopusbooks.co.uk

Distributed in the US by Hachette Book Group
1290 Avenue of the Americas, 4th and 5th Floors
New York, NY 10104

Distributed in Canada by Canadian Manda Group
664 Annette St., Toronto, Ontario, Canada M6S 2C8

Text copyright © Diana Henry 2019
Design and layout copyright © Octopus Publishing Group 2019
Photography copyright © Laura Edwards 2019

ISBN 978 1 78472 609 6

Printed and bound in China

10 9 8 7 6 5 4 3 2 1

Group Publishing Director: Denise Bates
Creative Director: Jonathan Christie
Photographer: Laura Edwards
Photographic assistant: Sam Harris
Design and Art Direction: Miranda Harvey
Editor: Lucy Bannell
Home Economist and Food Stylist: Joss Herd
Assistant Home Economist: India Whiley-Morton
Senior Production Manager: Katherine Hockley

The recipes in this book were all tested in Diana Henry's oven
on the convection setting, which—on her oven—equates to
about 50°F less than a conventional oven. All the conversions
to Fahrenheit were driven by this. Your oven may differ;
we recommend you check it with an oven thermometer.

For Amy Bryant, with love and thanks

ACKNOWLEDGMENTS

Huge thanks, yet again, to my team—Laura Edwards, Miranda Harvey, Lucy Bannell, and Joss Herd—for their perfectionism and tremendously hard work. Also to our assistant food stylist, India Whiley-Morton, and photographer's assistant Sam Harris. Never have so many roasting pans been washed by so few people for just one book. (And thank you, Sam, for displaying the best priorities by starting to organize the shoot lunch from 11am every day. You're the man.)

Extra thanks to Lucy Bannell on this title as she didn't just edit it but also tested some of the recipes. In the last stages—when I had a very ill child—I don't know what I would have done without you, Lucy.

Thanks also to the team at Octopus, my publisher Denise Bates, creative director Jonathan Christie, and Frances Johnson and Katherine Hockley in production.

I'd also like to thank ace Americanizer, Sarah Chamberlain, and Ann ffolliott for bringing her expertise.

My friend and fellow food writer Melissa Clark generously gave me her recipe for butterflied lamb with yogurt and herb sauce on page 193 (Melissa writes for *The New York Times* and you'll find her eminently cookable recipes on their website). Thanks also to Von Diaz for allowing me to use a slightly amended version of her wonderful dish, sweet and sour chicken and chorizo in adobo, from her book *Coconuts and Collards* (University Press of Florida). Chef Andrew Clarke from St Leonard's restaurant in London helped me to create a home cook-friendly version of his roast cabbage with XO crumbs. It's one of the best dishes on his menu, so this is especially generous.

I have spent decades picking up ceramics in a very ad hoc way, but for this book I actually tracked down some wonderful additions. Thank you to Jono Smart and Emily Stephen, and to Pottery West for knowing just what I needed and for their generosity. Netherton Foundry, makers of superb pans, your kindness knows no bounds. Thank you for pans, baking sheets, skillets, and for driving from Shropshire when it was needed.

All cookbooks depend on good suppliers. The food stylists and I would like to give a huge shout-out to Kent & Son's Butchers of St John's Wood and Humphrey's Butchers in Saffron Walden for getting us great meat, often at short notice.

Finally, a massive thanks to Amy Bryant, my editor at *The Sunday Telegraph,* to whom this book is dedicated, for years of sifting through ideas, spotting mistakes in recipes, and endless support, friendship and kindness.